THIN SPACES

RECOGNIZING WHEN GOD BREAKS THROUGH

JEFF JERNIGAN, PHD, BCPC, FAIS
NANCY JERNIGAN, PHD, LPF, LPC

WESTBOW
P R E S S®
A DIVISION OF THOMAS NELSON
& ZONDERVAN

WestBow Press books may be ordered through booksellers or by contacting:

WestBow Press
A Division of Thomas Nelson & Zondervan
1663 Liberty Drive
Bloomington, IN 47403
www.westbowpress.com
844-714-3454

Author photo by Katie Fechner of KFechPhotography

ISBN: 979-8-3850-1215-2 (sc)
ISBN: 979-8-3850-1216-9 (hc)
ISBN: 979-8-3850-1217-6 (e)

Library of Congress Control Number: 2023921399

Print information available on the last page.

WestBow Press rev. date: 1/15/2024

To Lt. Col. Daniel Jernigan,
son, husband, father, and marine; your journey is a part of ours
and a seed of inspiration behind these pages.
A better man cannot be found.

ACKNOWLEDGEMENTS

We would like to genuinely thank the WestBow Press editorial, production, and marketing teams. This book was significantly enhanced through their editorial expertise, creativity, and vision. We are very grateful for your teamwork.

Thank you to the many friends and family members who are contained in these stories. Your influence and inspiration in our lives is included throughout these pages. A special thank you to both our CCV small group and Bible Study who prayed for this project, supported us throughout the process and are included in this book.

The lives of our parents have influenced us and are contained in these stories. We want to honor and acknowledge how our parents inspired us. Each in their own way they have impacted this book.

ENDORSEMENTS

God is with us in our daily lives, and if we're attuned to Him, we will experience His presence in powerful and profound ways. That's an important reminder for all of us as followers of Christ, and that's the message of this encouraging book from Jeff and Nancy Jernigan.

Jim Daly,
President, Focus on the Family

A beautiful book that encourages the reader to look for and to listen to God and desire to encounter Him in the thin places. Jeff and Nancy share their hearts and their own personal journeys of "thin spaces" along the way. They desire to help you step into these thin spaces and experience your own unforgettable, life-altering God moments, in order to encourage and sustain you along your journey.

Kim Moeller,
National Christian Foundation, San Diego Area Director

As one of Jeff and Nancy's pastors for many years, I know them as faithful servants of God with a love for their family, church, and community. That faithfulness and love form the foundation for "Thin Spaces" – a book that will help you to see with practical and personal clarity how to connect with God in every circumstance of life.

Tom Holladay
Saddleback Church, Purpose Driven Training, P.E.A.C.E Plan
DrivetimeDevotions.com

It's often when we find and recognize our "thin space" that deep understanding comes from God. Jeff and Nancy taught me that sometimes our breakthroughs with God are found in the simplicity of life. A thin space is where heaven and earth seem to be closest. For me I find that what the Celtics taught over a thousand years ago about thin spaces is relevant in my pain and quiet surrender to God. You will love this book and it will help you draw closer to the Lord.

Jim Burns, PhD
President, HomeWord
Author of Have Serious Fun and Doing Life with Your Adult Children

Being close to God and feeling His presence is a place we all want to be. Over a thousand years ago, the Celtic Christians understood this concept well. They called it a thin place. Nancy and Jeff have laid out a pathway to help guide you to that 'thin place' today.

Greg Leith
CEO, Convene Corporation
www.convenenow.com

Jeff and Nancy bring out a unique approach in understanding how to recognize, test and grow in the ability to hear from God and the role this plays in our spiritual restoration. Recognizing how God breaks through our preconceived notions, our bias and stereotypes, and our uncertainty to make himself known to us is an art and discipline. God longs for a deep connection with every believer and this relationship brings wholeness of the soul.

Erik Rees
CEO, Jessie Rees Foundation

CONTENTS

INTRODUCTION

Thin spaces are gifts from God. This gift of his presence in our lives is as relevant today as in the beginning of time. We unwrap and explore this gift in the chapters to follow. How does God communicate to us? Why do we miss the message at times? Is it our imagination or personal desires that are giving us impressions? When it seems God is silent, how should we understand the silence? Where can I find God when I need his guidance? Is there some kind of test to determine if what we sense is really from God? Does God really want a personal relationship with me? In more than forty years of ministry, we have been asked these questions over and over again by people just like us from all over the world. More importantly, we have struggled with these questions as well.

Thin spaces is a term from early Celtic Christianity more than a thousand years ago, describing those places where God breaks through into our lives in a personal encounter. Some ascribe thin space status to a particular inspirational location, while others view locale as wherever it happens. I first remember hearing the term used by Tim Bohlke, founder and director of Rogue Journey, a Harbor Ministries event for pastors and Christian businessmen who want to finish well.

Nancy and I have a lot of thin spaces stories to tell you in this book. Our journey through life and ministry together has covered forty-two countries in forty years, many of which were considered risk zones at the time. Our ministry of healing, health, and restoration of people, teams, and organizations has focused on finishing well. We help guide people to solutions in life that produce thinking, feeling, and acting in ways that create healthy physical, social, and spiritual well-being.

Another term you will find used occasionally is *whispers.* Nothing mystical here, just a great word picture of how the Holy Spirit often gets our attention. We teach people how to listen for the whispers in the sense of the conversation Elijah had with God when fleeing Jezebel's vindictive wrath.

God did not speak in the storm, or the earthquake, or the fire.[1] He spoke in a low whisper, and Elijah heard it. It may even be a word spoken louder, as in the case of Isaiah instructing the people to listen to their teacher.[2] *Breakthrough* is a term most of us do not associate with personal encounters with God. Yet this is exactly what Isaiah was speaking about when he observed God was doing a new thing, bewildered a bit that no one seemed to perceive it even though it was breaking forth.[3]

The idea of whispered messages and supernatural breakthroughs may be off-putting to some. There was a time in my life this was certainly true for me. I am an engineer, pastor, hospital administrator, and board-certified mental health professional with a huge need for evidence-based insights due to a naturally skeptical nature. And then there was a breakthrough in my own life. Thin spaces have been misunderstood and ignored for years but nevertheless are still thin spaces.

The occasion was a middle-of-the-night need to move our platoon from one location to another immediately, with full packs and weapons. Already worn out and dehydrated, I was not doing well, falling behind and on the verge of collapse. The consequences of collapsing were unconscionable. At this point in my life, I was well churched and believed there was a God and Jesus was his Son but not much more. Crying out to God, I said, "God, if you are real, please help me!" The man behind me stepped up just off my left shoulder out of line of sight and helped lift my pack as we ran together.

When we arrived at our destination, I sought him out, or at least who I thought it was, and thanked him. He denied even getting close to me, describing his own struggles as nearly overwhelming. I asked around. Nobody helped me, some even saying they saw me running alone with no one around me. Befuddled, I chalked it up to the stress of the moment and walked away from the experience without so much as a thank you to anyone. It would be a number of years before I became a follower of Jesus Christ in the sense of a personal relationship and put the experience into new context. It would take longer to begin to recognize other thin spaces in my relationship with Christ and learning how to take ego out of evaluating authenticity. How do I know if this wasn't just wishful imagination, bias, trauma-induced stress, or some other human factor? How do I test this experience to know it was valid and true? There are commonsense, practical, and replicable ways to test reality and draw your own conclusions.

In our ministry, we teach people how to listen to the whispers and recognize the thin spaces. Both continue to be part of our life and walk in Christ, some fitting into normal life almost unnoticed and some far more arresting, as you will see. We also have come to understand that God is constantly doing two things in our lives: deconstructing outworn ideas and convictions while at the same time creating new understanding and beliefs. Whispers and thin spaces are part of this process for everyone. Our world changes around us all the time as a function of history. Nothing stays the same in our lives, and we move forward with these changes as well. If we are not learning, transforming, maturing even as adults, it is less likely we will notice the whispers or recognize a thin space when they occur since we really are not looking for them or the changes they may bring. The problem of insensitivity is addressed from a very practical perspective in this book as well. Nancy likes to say, "If you are doing the work God approves, life is an adventure!" Here, she is to introduce herself.

As an ordained pastor, executive coach, master life coach, leadership development trainer and teacher, I am passionate about developing and multiplying leaders and teams at churches and nonprofit organizations. From a very young age, I had a passion to encourage and teach others. As early as the fifth grade, I would "teach" the neighbor children sitting in the basement using old desks rescued from a local school. Years later, while finalizing my bachelor of science degree in education and continuing my career in education and marketing, I felt a strong desire to surrender my career to God, confident I wanted my work to be guided by God, serving kingdom purposes. After spending some years at Christianity Today and then Focus on the Family and moving from Chicago to Southern California, I recall a very important breakthrough moment and an important thin space experience.

At midnight one evening, I was awakened by what I knew was God telling me to "Go" and leave a happy, contented life in Southern California and make the move with Focus on the Family to Colorado Springs, Colorado. I did not want to leave this newfound paradise (compared to Chicago) with year-round great weather, new friends, and sandy beaches for an unknown life in Colorado. So, at midnight, I called the one person who would pick up my call and not be mad about being awakened at this very late hour. My sister Cindy listened to me share the story of my encounter with God and immediately said to me, "Great, I think this is where you are going to meet your husband." She went on to say, "I agree with God, Nancy. Go to Colorado Springs!" Still complaining, I did go, and I did meet my hero and best friend, Jeff. In due time, we fell in love and were married and have shared many adventures for many years now.

The scripture I kept on the top of my desk and looked at practically every day for years leading up to meeting my husband was "And I will lead the blind by ways they do not know, along unfamiliar paths I will guide them; I will turn the darkness into light before them and make the rough places smooth. These are the things I do, and I will not forsake them"[4] (Isaiah 42:16 NIV).

Little did I know this scripture would not only carry me through this unforeseen change but be an encouragement to myself and many others in times of stress, tension, and difficulty. It remains for me a beautiful description of how God carries us when our hearts, souls, and minds need the stability that only the one, true God can offer. When we need to be brought to a place of healing and health, God restores us to a place of stability where we can move forward serving the purposes he has ordained for our life.

There are a lot of terms related to one another we will unpack in this book. Here are a few important ones. Restoration, as used here, has in mind restoring someone to a former state of usefulness in order to serve the purpose for which they were designed.[5] Restoration is a transformative process involving a number of elements. Restoration includes reconciliation, which requires breaking down the perceptions and boundaries that separate us from health and healing experiences. Ultimately, what separates us from one another and from God needs to be put back together and restored. This is one of Jesus's main goals for all of us, indeed all of creation.[6] Restoration and reconciliation require a healthy sense of self and an understanding of our need for healing of our soul and peace for our mind. No more swimming upstream with no boat and no paddle when we are called upon to do hard things.

Repentance requires a change in direction in habit and thinking. If not replaced quickly by new direction, it is likely we will fall back into the rut we just escaped. Renewal, to make new again, requires knowing what the hole in our soul is and how the Holy Spirit fills up what has leaked out, so we don't have to find our own solutions.[7] Recovery allows us to regain purpose and meaning in our relationships and our work.

A life of restoration, reconciliation, repentance, renewal, and recovery involves significant transformational work. We need the help and guidance of the Holy Spirit and the many thin spaces to move us forward in the restorative process. All of these are a part of restoration, which is what this book is about. Here is Jeff's summary of Psalm 23 based on the ESV.

Psalm 23 is a psalm of restoration featuring these components:
The Lord is my shepherd.
He meets all of my needs.
He gives me rest.
He knows what I need.
He fills up my soul.
He guides me.
He protects me.
He grants me favor.
He fills my life with blessing.
Surely goodness and mercy shall follow me all the days of my life.

1

ROLE OF THE HOLY SPIRIT

A VOICE BEHIND ME (JEFF) asked, "Where is Danny?" I turned and looked across two adjacent backyards and saw no one. Looking down to the pond about twenty-five yards away, I was caught off guard by a sudden sense of dread. Danny was two years old and playing with other children under adult supervision. Only Danny wasn't there. Looking over the pond, my eyes were drawn to a spot in the water just a short distance from the beach. Suddenly, I knew Danny was under water in that exact spot. Like a maniac, I was out of the beach chair, charging the pond as if it were the enemy. Splashing through the water until it was over my waist, I stopped, and seeing nothing in the cloudy water, I thrust my hand down and was surprised when Danny's hair filled my hand. Alarmed as only a father can be, I nearly cried with relief and fear.

Quickly pulling him up, I could tell he wasn't breathing. His eyes were open, fixed, and totally dilated. Lips and fingertips were blue. Taking him to shore, I began CPR. In the background, I could hear someone calling an ambulance. There was no response. It took me a moment to realize my worst fear was being realized in front of me. Kneeling next to my son in the sand, I picked him up and held him to my chest. I thanked God for the gift of his life, thinking he was dead. At that moment, I felt his heartbeat against my chest! Danny recovered completely without any side effects. Today, he has a wonderful family, and he has blessed us with two grandchildren. He is successful in his career serving our country, and he is a follower of Jesus Christ. Thank you, Lord!

Was that the Holy Spirit who spoke? Was that who filled me with apprehension and directed me to the very place where Danny was drowning? Did we all just see a miracle, or was what happened just a syncope, or simply the result of a loss in blood pressure?

Many years had passed between the time, as a young marine, I was seemingly helped out of trouble and into safety and this event at the pond. By then, I had become a Christian. I was serving in church and volunteering with a college campus Christian organization, working with students. There had been a few tugs toward full-time ministry, which I dutifully ignored and stuffed away. That was not part of the career mapped out in my imagination. But I did have some encounters with God between these two events. Like when God spoke words in my mind telling me I was his servant, and it was his opinion that counted, not mine. And when I was asked by a friend to pray for his daughter on the table in surgery for an emergency procedure to save her life. I claimed a promise from scripture, prayed, and headed right to the hospital.

When I got to the hospital some hours later, she was being discharged. Evidently, when the surgeon was ready to begin—the problem disappeared! No test could reveal anything wrong in spite of previous testing confirming a malignant ruptured appendix.

But was there more than answered prayers or a sense of God

pressing upon me in response to a selfish pursuit of a planned career choice? Are there more direct and personal ways God connects with us? Am I missing something because I am not paying attention? Or worse, do I not want to hear from God when I don't think I will like the conversation? This is where the Holy Spirit comes into the picture.

Nancy was young in her life in Christ as well, but she had no doubt or question about God's desire to have a relationship with people. She had no questions about God's ability and desire to connect with us in meaningful ways. She just didn't know how to make that connection at a deeper level until she learned to listen.

Thin spaces have taken place in our (Nancy) lives since we were very young. We are just not always conscious of God's presence, yet they are a part of our spiritual development. A desire to have a listening ear for the whispers of God develops our relationship with him, and it grows our ability to hear when he is speaking to us directly. God has been communicating his love, presence, and care for us in a variety of ways since our life began. As we mature and develop in our relationship with God, we gradually hear his voice more clearly and more directly. These breakthrough moments add to the ways he communicates with us and give us more specific direction, comfort, and assurance.

God created us in his own image, including a desire and ability to communicate with him in the context of a vibrant relationship.[8] Like Abraham, Elijah, Isaiah, Deborah, Priscilla, and so many more, God speaks to us in a way he knows is attuned to our temperament, gifts, maturity, and experiences. My (Nancy) prayer is to walk so closely with God that it is like my toes are at his figurative heals. Paul, in the book of Romans, explains how we are to live according to the Spirit, setting our minds on God's purposes and desires of the Spirit. Our desire to hear from God begins with a heart to know God better, understand his ways, and play an active part in his kingdom's purposes. This was at the core of my prayer when I sat down and wanted to hear more often from God. It was during this time of desiring to hear more from God I took part in a two-day life plan process. My (Nancy) life plan coach, Amy, guided me through a very specific process of looking back over my life, assessing my gifts, and planning for the future. An important takeaway from our time together was when Amy encouraged me to spend more time with God, and we discussed what this spiritual discipline would look like for me moving forward.

So right after completing the two-day life plan, I committed to spending twenty minutes a day sitting quietly and listening to God. Each twenty-minute period looked slightly different, yet usually I would start by reading a scripture, time in prayer for my concerns, and then I would just say, "God, I am here to listen to you. I am your servant, and do with this time as you desire." Then I would stop, listen, and then sit quietly for twenty minutes. Oftentimes, I would not hear much, and I would keep repeating, "God, I am here. Speak. Your servant is listening." Many times, I would hear what Jeff and I call *impressions*. I would sense a word, thought, or question from God and write it down. I would keep praying, "Lord, open my eyes and ears to hear from you." During these times, I often felt encouraged and inspired. These times were fruitful and fulfilling. On a few occasions, I would even catch a vision. I would see a picture of what God was communicating to me.

It was everyday life stuff, not a mysterious vision. As I continued listening to God for twenty minutes at a time, I noticed I had more patience and strength to continue this process. I would get excited for my time with him. Many days, I missed or did not take the whole twenty minutes, but other days, I spent more time with him and would even return later in the day to pray about a very important concern. I would continue to pray and ask God to teach me in this process according to his will and ways. Sometimes

I had a specific question to ask God, and I would spend the time on specific subject matter, asking God a particular question. As time went on, Jeff and I would pray, "Lord, teach us even while we sleep." Sometimes we would wake up having resolved something that had been concerning us for a long time. And we realized God was indeed teaching us and showing us an outcome while we slept.

This spiritual discipline of listening to God is at the heart of my relationship with God. It brings the knowledge of scripture into my practical day-to-day life with God. Having this intimate relationship and conversation with God is now the highlight of my day. It is the most thrilling part of my life in God. Being drawn to God in conversation by the power of the Holy Spirit living in me is the energy that guides me each and every day. The Holy Spirit was intended to be our gift, communicating God's wisdom and guidance directly to our hearts so we can "walk in the Spirit" throughout our lives. The Spirit who dwells in us is the one who delivers the gift of whispers, visions, words of encouragement, and so much more.[9]

So when you and I desire to hear from God on a myriad of topics, issues, and concerns, we pause our busy minds—stop and listen—to hear and make note of the message God is conveying to us. Throughout this book, we will sprinkle insights and tips. One of the most critical and important disciplines we would like to share is to write down or record in a journal what you believe God has spoken to your heart. There are many reasons why recording what he says is important, yet one of the most critical reasons is so you can go back and recall what God really said. You may even need to pray and ask God to make clear his message because we all tend to put our own filter over what we think God meant by the message he delivered. You will hear from Jeff and me that many times it is a process over time to truly understand what God is trying to convey to us from the words he speaks. Listening to God with a heart to understand includes grasping what God meant by his words.

This kind of listening is not special knowledge or difficult to comprehend. The message of scripture about the Holy Spirit's role in our lives is simple and clear, easily comprehended, and of great practical help. Most of us simply have not been taught much about the Holy Spirit, other than he is the third person in the Trinity. Here are some basic truths that have enabled us to hear the whispers, recognize the thin spaces, and sustain us in our journey.[10]

1. We receive the Holy Spirit when we receive Christ. We have all of the Holy Spirit, lacking nothing of his presence or power.[11]

2. The Holy Spirit helps us understand the teachings freely given to us by God. This includes the Bible, experiencing God's presence in our life and circumstances, as well as visions, dreams, and miracles that may be part of his relationship with us. God will communicate with us in the context of our language, social paradigm, and culture because he wants to be understood. He also wants us to test everything to be sure it is not our bias, expectations, or desires spinning his message to what we long to hear.[12]

3. The Holy Spirit is present in a corporate way when we fellowship together with other believers.[13] He draws us together, provides insight, and influences us all toward greater Christlikeness.

4. The Holy Spirit brings light into the darkness of our lives at just the right time. We are to be filled with the Holy Spirit.[14] This filling is grammatically not a pouring of something into an empty vessel but rather an igniting of something already there that fills us to overflowing from the inside out.

These are a few basic concepts. There is so much more to the role of the Holy Spirit in us and in the world, beginning with leading the nonbeliever to a place of choice to make regarding Christ. Is he your personal Savior, a prophet, a legend, someone to reject or receive into your life? For a Christian, the Holy Spirit's role continues as he draws us on to greater spiritual maturity. Paul calls this "participation in the Spirit" (communion or fellowship), something we all mutually enjoy, which influences our lives in ways the world can see and respond to with favor.[15] The Holy Spirit is not a substance to fill an empty receptacle. He is a person living in us who influences, guides, helps, and controls us. When we receive Christ, we have all of the Holy Spirit for eternity.

Without the Holy Spirit, we will not experience the peace that passes all understanding.[16]

This kind of peace is not accidental; it is carefully crafted from wisdom we do not possess on our own.[17] Without the Holy Spirit, there is no corrective to the impression many of us had growing up of God and Jesus Christ being autocratic, dictatorial, just waiting for an opportunity to punish us.[18] The first two words God uses to describe himself are "merciful and gracious."[19] The first two words Jesus uses to describe himself are "gentle and lowly."[20] God is for us, not against us. Christ died for us that we might have new life characterized by inner peace in the absence of fear, giving us the right to become beloved members of his family.[21] The Holy Spirit is the one who introduces us and places us into this family.[22]

The result of lack of clear teaching about the role of the Holy Spirit also shows up in controversy about spiritual gifts. What are they? Does everyone have them? How do they work? Can they be taken away? Why do we have them? Here are some foundational truths that will help guide you as you find your own answers to these questions in the scripture.

1. Spiritual gifts are given to Christians to enable their functioning in the worldwide body of Christ, or Church with a capital C.[23] They are key to our function in the world as Christians. The word Paul chose to use here for *function* speaks to a skill, practice, or occupation that is unique in an extraordinary manner beyond a skill or talent and that moves God's purposes forward.[24] There are a number of gifts identified in scripture but no definitive statement that these are the only gifts. God places people with different gifts wherever he chooses to place them.[25] Some Bible translations use "placed," "arranged," "set," or "put" to describe this action of placing people. There are two words in New Testament language that can be used for this kind of placement. One means to place hierarchal, one over others and so on, like an organizational chart. The other word means to place people equally, on a level plane, like chess pieces on a chess board. This is the word used here. Though we may have different gifts and different roles, we all have equal value.

2. Our gifts are designed to be used for the benefit of others and not to be used to exploit opportunities for ourselves.[26] Paul uses the term *common good*, describing the use of gifts that, by definition, excludes personal gain.

3. The Bible contains instructions for the proper use of all gifts and does not leave the way spiritual gifts are exercised up to our imaginations.[27]

Some gifts lend themselves more directly to leadership. These are sometimes called the equipping gifts, where equipping is a function and not a person.[28] These roles primarily have to do with shepherding people in their maturing walk with Christ and equipping them for the work of ministry in ways that grow the church and promote unity. Sometimes we forget that it is the Holy Spirit who anoints people for leadership in ministry, not us. I know I have lost sight of this truth more than once.

Pastors, ministry executives, and lay leaders are always looking for more leaders. The assumption is disciples can become disciple makers and eventually senior leaders in ministry. When those recruited to this paradigm don't meet whatever the standard for a multitalented Christian leader is in an organization, they are set aside, looked down upon, or considered a failure because they don't live up to our standard. They are not living up to their potential. They evidently are not equippers and therefore of less interest to us. Thin space experiences are not always dramatic, exciting, and positive. Sometimes they are a rebuke and correction to our erroneous thinking. On a church men's fishing retreat in the Sierras, I (Jeff) had one of these corrective experiences. I was the church's senior pastor.

We had hiked into the mountains for a weeklong camping and fly-fishing retreat. The group included men from our church and friends they had been encouraged to invite. One of these guests was a man who also brought his two sons along. As time went by, it was clear to me that he and his wife were doing a great job of raising these boys. They seemed to have a great marriage and were an involved part of their church community. He was a scout leader for the Cub Scout Pack sponsored by their church. He also was an assistant coach on his sons' sports teams and led a Sunday school class. His wife and he were in a small group that met weekly for Bible study, and she sang in the choir. He was a fireman with a flexible schedule and had a great reputation at work and in his church. When I queried him about considering other leadership responsibilities like leading a men's ministry, leading a small group in their home, or leading outreach efforts for their church, he was clearly put off and explained a lot of people were pushing him to step up in regard to ministry leadership, including becoming an elder in the church. He made it clear he believed he was right where God wanted him to be. End of conversation.

The next day was a day off from fishing. I took a hike and found a quiet place to read my Bible and reflect. My disappointment and frustration with people that could step up in ministry leadership but chose not to kept coming to mind. As I prayed about this problem of people unwilling to respond to invitations to grow in their leadership abilities, I said out loud, "What is wrong with this man!" meaning, of course, the scout leader in our group. Immediately the air chilled, a profound sense of presence surrounded me, and I sensed a clear message that there was *nothing* wrong with him, but there was something very wrong with me. Then the Holy Spirit took me to school. Coming back to camp from that encounter, this is what I wrote in my journal:

> Day Four: reading in Deuteronomy 10 today. 10.12 ESV talks about what the Lord requires of anyone. Fear or reverence for God, walk in his ways, love him, serve him wholeheartedly.[29] If we can help people do this, it is enough, it is all that God requires. This is the focus of 'Consider Your Ways:'[30] these four fundamentals. Some can and should go further. But it is a mistake to try to take everyone further. This has been pointed out to me in getting to know George[31] and his two boys. My temptation is to recruit him to leadership. But he will not respond. He doesn't want to and senses no calling for God. He has no time left over in his day. He is happy where he is spiritually. As far as I can tell, he fears God, walks in his ways, loves him, and serves him though church and community

involvement. If God does not touch good people like this with an appetite for more, who am I to say they are falling short? After all, they are doing all that God requires!

I recognized a need immediately to stop playing the junior holy spirit and let the genuine Holy Spirit do the recruiting. The Holy Spirit leads people into a decision to accept Christ, gives them gifts, helps them understand the teachings of God, and is instrumental in calling them to a function and role in the body of Christ. We are called to walk by the Spirit and be led by the Holy Spirit.[32] We have our job, and the Holy Spirit has his job. Some people are called into leadership roles and respond to the Holy Spirit's prompting by seeking out leadership development. Nancy has no end of women being drawn to her for encouragement, coaching, mentoring, and leadership development. The Holy Spirit calls them, and she disciples them. Here is a great example.

As Jeff indicated, leadership development involves a call from the Holy Spirit, an appropriate gift mix, a willing heart, and someone to come alongside to inspire, train, and offer opportunities. Morgan is one of the most inspiring leadership stories unfolding even as we write this manuscript. Morgan clearly has a leadership call on her life and has a heart to serve God from a young age. A number of years ago, we were both serving at a large church in Southern California in women's ministry. She was on the women's leadership intern team while finishing up her college degree, and I was overseeing leadership development for women's ministry and women's small group leaders. We were preparing for a large event and meeting with a small group of women leaders in my home. Jeff and I had received a phone call asking us if we were available to open our home to a specific church intern to live with us throughout their internship at this church. We had responded with an excited and wholehearted yes, knowing God already made it clear our hearts had been drawn together in a rare way regarding this intern, and we were already starting to feel like family.

Flash back to the women's leadership meeting in our home. Everyone else had left except Morgan, as she indicated she had a question for me. She wanted to ask me face-to-face about the opportunity to live with us during her internship while she finished her college education. I answered with a heartfelt yes, already seeing her maturity, the way she handled ministry responsibilities, work, and life situations. It was the beginning of many hours of ministry discussions, doing life together, and Saturday mornings filled with hot coffee, tasty treats, opened Bibles, anticipating God to guide and speak to us as we discussed biblical concepts applicable to living life in this world. Many profound moments were experienced with Morgan, Jeff, and I around our breakfast table. In addition, she and I served side by side on many occasions.

On one occasion, we were able to teach together at a women's small group leadership training session. We planned, studied, and prepared together as well as separately for this diverse group of women ranging in ages from Morgan's age to my age and older. This is an example of "generational leadership multiplication" illustrated as "A - AB - B." The mentor teaches and models (A), helps the mentee learn and do (AB), and continues to encourage once the mentee (B) is leading well on their own. The memories Morgan and I had together were and are priceless and continue today even though we are two thousand miles apart at the moment of writing this chapter. By the time the last word was written in this book, we found ourselves living ten minutes away from each other and serving in the same church in Chandler, Arizona.

Morgan clearly has a pastoral leadership call on her life and is serving as a pastor today, called and confirmed by the church leadership where she serves. She shepherds many in their spiritual walk with wisdom, insight, gentleness, maturity, and kindness. She is a rare gem.

2

DISCIPLINES OF PRESENCE

GOD IS WITH US ALWAYS! He is ever present, all knowing, always working and moving in our lives. When we are not aware of him, it is a problem with our focus, not his presence. So, when we are developing an ear to hear God, we are strengthening our senses to understand the ways God is speaking to us and present with us.[33]

God will and is speaking to us in a variety of ways and circumstances every day. When we read scriptures such as Matthew 28:20 (NIV), God is declaring he is with us always. Earlier in the verse, God asks us to teach others to observe all the things God is doing and to obey everything God has commanded us.[34] Part of the emphasis is to observe, share, and understand God's presence and his ways. Developing our ability to listen and hear God's voice is a process that continues over our entire lives.

Listening and hearing are two different steps. Taking time to be quiet or listen to God is one step. Actually hearing from God is another. My (Nancy) twenty minutes in the morning during my quiet times turned into specific times throughout the day when I would ask God to guide me or answer a question. Another example is listening during church services or spiritual conferences. Church services are appropriate times to pray and ask for direction or present a specific request to God. Then if your service allows for a quiet time, take some time and listen for an answer right there in church. Ask the Holy Spirit to make the answer clear and confirm God's message. Jeff and I have heard various impressions, convictions, and words conveying something during church services, which were confirmed later. We both recently heard a message from God that more change is coming in our lives. When a couple hears a similar message from God, it is worth pondering and seeking further insight. This is a highlight of our day when we each hear a message and we can share with each other our sense of what God is saying. We often try to write it down immediately so we can reflect on it and ask God to confirm the message.

Often, we may have prayed for a specific situation in the middle of the day, and then we become aware of an answer to our prayer many hours or days later. God chooses the time and place to answer our prayers. Sometimes the time or place is important, and other times God has our attention and chooses the time and place and we are not sure why. Our backyard looks out to a long vista of trees, homes, hills, and mountains. It is a good place to sit, ponder, pray, and listen for God to speak regarding pressing issues. Sometimes just being quiet is good for our soul, and we do not hear anything in particular.

Our posture of a surrendered heart, open and available to God's will, sets us up to hear God's message. The attitude of availability is huge. Do not take your surrendered heart lightly. This is a critical part of hearing from God. Preparing ourselves to be able to hear any message God chooses to share is a very important part of our relationship with God. As we are writing this manuscript, Jeff and I have surrendered where we live to God's will. We have prayed in agreement together and are prepared and desiring to move according to God's ways. Our attitude throughout the day, whether at work or play, is essential to the process of hearing from God. Are we stubborn or open in a certain situation? Are we flexible or demanding? Ponder your attitude throughout the day and pray for God to shift your thinking to be open, surrendered, and obedient to calls from God.[35]

Once again, our thoughts throughout the day are an important part of our relationship with God and hearing from God. When I sense I am holding tightly on to a desire or outcome, as soon as I start to notice this attitude in my life, I do my best to acknowledge it, open my hands in an outward manner, pray, and surrender it to God. Showing God I am open to his will helps my heart to follow. Some desires are harder than others to release to God's will. Asking God to speak and reveal his will helps our hearts to shift and align with God's desires and ways.

The disciples came to Jesus one day asking Jesus why he spoke in parables. This happened on a number of occasions, and at one time Jesus was talking about the kingdom of God. He was teaching the disciples that believers have the ability to see and perceive as well as to hear and understand, although those outside the kingdom of God (unbelievers) may not hear, see, or perceive.[36] This ability to see and perceive or hear and understand is because of the Holy Spirit living in us. The Holy Spirit is the one who reveals the ways of God and opens our spiritual eyes and ears to understand.

Taking time to hear from God through the work of the Holy Spirit is a discipline that will reveal so many of God's ways, both in reading the Word of God and in hearing from God. As you read God's Word, pray, "Lord open my eyes to see what you have for me to understand in scripture." Pray for insights, revelations, and answers to your prayers through God's Word. Your desire to understand God's Word along with a surrendered attitude will enhance and amplify your time with God as well as affect your ability to hear from God.

Awareness of God's daily presence grows on you. When God called me (Jeff) to be a missionary and pastor, it was over a period of time at different intervals and more like a prodding or reminder than a message. There came a time later in life that sensing his presence was a habit, to the point if I rose from my daily devotions too soon, I would be tugged at the elbow as a reminder that I might have been done with the conversation, but he was not. Time to sit back down to pray and listen some more. Experiencing the presence of God is not a formula with steps to follow or conditions to fulfill. It is forged over time in our relationship with Jesus Christ. Knowing him is the key, and recognizing his presence flows naturally out of that knowing.

This experience of knowing him, having a personal relationship with the living God, is developed out of spiritual disciplines.[37] Richard Foster in *Celebration of Discipline* divides these into three categories: inward, outward, and corporate. Together they represent time spent in daily devotions, Bible study, and reflection. Meditation and prayer are inward disciplines as well. Outward disciplines include simplicity, solitude, and service to others, whether it be family, friends, or church or other ministry, or even strangers. Things we do together like worship, counseling, fellowship, and celebrations are examples of corporate disciplines. The term *discipline* shouldn't scare you off. It simply means you have practiced something enough that it has become natural in your behavior.

As a very young believer, I had the mistaken idea that God wanted to take some things away from me. There certainly were some habits needing change in my life. Enough wrong choices and bad decisions over time create baggage for all of us. But this idea of a personal relationship with Jesus Christ isn't about taking away. Jesus only willingly takes what people are willing to give. It is always a choice. Jesus wants to give us an abundant life.[38] *Abundant* refers to an experience over and above what we could think of or ask for, regardless of our situation, good or not so good. The disciplines of presence teach us about our Savior, introduce us to how he thinks and acts toward us, and guide us into right living.

This guidance comes in many forms. God allowed me to experience the desert of failure for a time, all the while telling me mindfully he was there with me. On another occasion, he sent a friend to me with a message of encouragement. God awakened him early Sunday morning and sent him to our church, which he had visited only on a few occasions. After the service, he stopped me on the way out and give me the message, "God has watched you rise before long before sunrise and has seen your tears and heard your prayers." There was more to the message, but what stood out to me is that no one, including my wife, had any idea I was getting up in the wee hours, going to the other side of the house, and unloading my concerns on God. How did my friend know? Bottom line, his word of encouragement to me from God was to press on with what I was doing. God is in control, and everything is going to be all right. And it was. On another occasion, when I was angry and resentful about one of our staff's disloyalty and betrayal, God spoke out loud and said, "I have shown you nothing but grace, kindness, and mercy throughout your life. You should do the same for others." And I did. Most of the time, guidance comes in the form of understanding God's Word in the Bible, or an impression driven home by the Holy Spirit, or the consensus of counsel from trusted Christian friends. But also, when it is warranted, in more dramatic ways.

My (Jeff) brother and I were given a small crystal radio by our father when we were in grade school. It was something out of his past as a boy and fascinated us. Built of a few parts on a small block of wood, it uses a Galena crystal to produce sound when tuned to a radio frequency. You must lean close and listen carefully to hear the tiny sound since it is not amplified in any way. When the weather changed from hot to cold or back, the station would drift away and become full of static. We would have to tune the radio to find the clear station again. If we left the radio alone for too long, the station would disappear altogether and be even more difficult to tune in. It was one of those use-it-or-lose-it times.

Staying tuned in spiritually is a lot like using a crystal radio. When we are regularly in the Word, praying, having regular devotions, fellowshipping with other Christians, in other words practicing the spiritual disciplines, it is easy to stay on station, so to speak. But when we ignore these habits, we easily become detuned and wonder where God went. He did not go anywhere; we did. God is waiting on-station for us to tune in again. Just like me and my brother, we sometimes just stop listening. When this happens spiritually, God stops talking.[39] Creating time and space for a relationship takes discipline. It only takes the tyranny of the urgent to be busy and distracted.

There are other reasons we may drift away as well.[40] Sometimes we resist the promptings of the Holy Spirit to the point of disobedience, leading to a silent presence.[41] It is the Holy Spirit who convinces and guides, opening the eyes of the heart with insight and understanding.[42] If we refuse to respond long enough, we are in effect quenching the Holy Spirit.[43] If we have a significant relationship with someone and for some reason stop responding to them, they will eventually go silent on us. This has happened to all of us at one time or another. Sometimes it may be our unconscious habits pushing us away. When this happens, it is called habituation.

Habituation occurs when we experience a decrease in response to something or someone because of repetition. For example, the beeping of your car's proximity alarm when you are too close to another car in the parking lot. Fenders still get crunched all the time because we tend to tune out that frequently occurring warning to the point of not hearing it. Ignoring the sound becomes an unconscious habit. We do this with the Holy Spirit as well. This is especially true if we are practicing the disciplines of presence as if it were a duty, a formulaic requirement that becomes rote like the workings of a machine. Sometimes our unconscious bias can push us away when something we hear or believe about church or our Christian brothers and sisters triggers a critical spirit in our hearts. This is one reason why we are challenged in scripture to not be judgmental and to always search the scripture like a good Berean to determine how to respond rather than using our own yardstick to measure others.[44] De-habituation is a process of learning how to listen to the Holy Spirit without bias and without looking for a formula for how to listen. This is a mutual relationship we want to invest ourselves in for the long haul. Relationships take time and our investment in the relationship in order to be meaningful.

It is in the context of our relationship with Jesus Christ that the Holy Spirit leads us into encounters with God. This not only leads to our experience of thin spaces but also enables us to benefit from those same experiences others have that act like a stone dropped in a pond. The ripple effect reaches us and provides some unrelated insight intended for only us, even though God was showing up for them. In God's economy, nothing is wasted, and your experiences in this regard will additionally impact the lives of others for his purposes and glory. Here are a few examples.

Gerald (not his real name) and his family lived across the street from us. He was a bank employee working in Los Angeles. His job included commercial business development, which took him all over the city. One afternoon after an appointment, on his way home, he stopped at an ATM. The woman in front of him dropped something as she rumbled through her very large purse, and he picked it up and handed it to her with a brief exchange of "Thank you" and "You are welcome." Gerald took his turn at the ATM as the woman walked away and then returned to his car.

Getting in and reaching for the door, he was suddenly surprised that the door wouldn't move. Looking at the door, he followed a hand holding it open up until he saw the weapon pointed at him from two feet away. He widened his view in astonishment as he realized the car was surrounded by police officers, all with weapons drawn and pointed at him. They were ordering him to get out of the car, hands in view, and get on the ground. He thought he was being profiled and was just about to stand up and give the police a lecture. Then he noticed me standing next to the policeman at the door and just stared.

Now, it wasn't me. I was ninety miles away at the time. However, as Gerald told the story, it evidently looked like me and sounded like me. Or, rather what he saw looked and sounded like me when I said, "God is in control, and everything is going to be all right." I was not there and had no idea what he saw, or thought he saw and heard. However, it possibly saved his life.

This was a phrase I repeated often in church when times were hard and nothing was working the way it should. It stopped Gerald in his tracks, and he remained still and calm. Evidently, the woman at the ATM was the girlfriend of a known violent gang leader. When the police followed her and witnessed the brief interaction at the ATM, they thought Gerald was the one they were looking for. They told Gerald, once his true identity had been confirmed, if he had stood up and confronted them, he would have been shot multiple times. None of them could see his hands, his appearance and car matched who they were looking for, and the person they were looking for was a violent criminal known for shooting first.

I am grateful Gerald told me about his experience. It was fresh in his mind, having just occurred. As he pulled into his driveway, he spotted me mowing my lawn and came immediately across the street to tell me what had happened. We were both very grateful he was not harmed, and I was grateful he had an encounter with God. The skeptic in me was tempted to chalk it up to an imaginative subconscious response to trauma. However, it was too specific to ignore. To this day, I do not know what happened to Gerald, only that it was a very present help in time of need as the scriptures promise.[45] But I do know how it helped me.

This came at a time when forward movement had stalled out in our work and ministry. I felt like my words were bouncing off unhearing walls, that no one was paying attention or even listening. That these words, "God is in control, and everything is going to be all right," were heard and made a difference in someone's life were like ripples in a pond. Gerald's experience reached out and gave me assurance that God was aware and engaged not only in Geraldss's life but my life as well.

On another occasion, my mother was standing all alone at the service counter in a hospital pharmacy. She had leaned over the counter and called out, but no one came. It was a large, empty room partially filled with chairs for people waiting to have their prescriptions filled. Only, no one was there, and she felt terribly alone and afraid. You see, she had just come downstairs from an appointment with her doctor, where she learned she had terminal cancer and not long to live. I wish I could tell you that she recovered, that everything was going to be all right. She didn't recover and passed as expected at the time appointed. However, something extraordinary happened along the way that changed absolutely everything.

While she was standing at the counter, she sensed someone walking up next to her. When she turned around, there was a woman standing there she had not heard come in to the still empty room. The woman, as my mother told me the story, had the kindest face and gentlest manner she had ever experienced in anyone. This stranger shared the Gospel without introduction and without preamble, while Mom listened politely. A voice from behind the counter said, "Can I help you?" My mother turned to acknowledge her, and when she turned immediately back to the woman she had been speaking to, she was gone. The room was still empty. Mom asked the pharmacist if they knew who she was talking to. They did not, and they did not notice her leaving either, busy with opening the register and logging in.

Some days later when we were together, Mom asked, "Who was that person? Was it God? Was it an angel? Why did they do that?" My sister and I had been concerned for some time about her spirituality. Certainly a churched person, did she have a personal relationship with Jesus Christ? That is, was her knowledge of God academic or something she had learned? Or was her faith personal and invested in a person, not just an idea. She was always ambivalent at that point in our conversation. I told her honestly that I did not know who the person was. As to why, I simply told her, "God loves you." Not long after that conversation, she passed away. Joyfully, my sister told me that Mom had resolved her doubts before she was gone and had placed her faith and trust in Jesus Christ.

The ripple for me in that story is a cautionary note. Again, I was not there and do not know what happened in that pharmacy. But something did happen, and it created a breakthrough for Mom. The cautionary note is a reminder that we are not in charge of salvation. We cannot convince anyone of our faith, we cannot judge the correctness of their confession, and we cannot make a faith decision for them, as much as we may like to do so. For me, her story assured me that God is in control, and everything is going to be all right regardless of the outcome.

My (Nancy) sister Cindy and I talk almost every week and sometimes a number of times during the week. We share spiritual lessons and significant scriptures we are reading and encourage each other in our faith journey. Often, when we have a significant God moment or breakthrough, we call each other to share the details and process our learnings as spiritual confidants. One of these such times, Cindy called to share how God had broken through and saved her life from a serious accident.

She was out running errands when she was entering an intersection on a green light and was about to proceed when, as she tells the story, she heard a voice say, "Look to the left!" She looked over her left shoulder and saw a car speeding through the intersection. Noticing the car headed in her direction gave her just enough time to stop suddenly and not proceed through the green light. She arrived at her destination and took a deep breath and pondered how the voice she heard was God warning her and saving her life. She called to recount the story and share how this not only potentially saved her life but encouraged her walk with God and strengthened her trust in a God who intercedes on her behalf. The ripple for me is every time she tells the story, recalls the details, and is reminded how God breaks through in our everyday life, I too am encouraged by God's presence and engagement in the details of our ordinary days. It brings me much comfort that God cares for my sister, one of the most important people in my life.

Sharing these stories with one another helps us remember and recall God's active presence in our lives. Just as God told Joshua to take twelve men and twelve stones after passing over the Jordan River and create a memorial in the place where God worked a mighty miracle in ushering the Israelites into the Promised Land.

God told them, "When your children ask in time to come, 'What do those stones mean to you?' Then you shall tell them that the waters of the Jordan were cut off before the ark of the covenant of the Lord"[46] (Joshua 4:1–10 ESV). The lesson is simple. Do not forget the miracles of God and what God has done in your life. Share your stories with others and with your children. These stories have the potential to bring numerous ripple effects for generations to come, allowing the miracles of God to strengthen the faith of many. "So that all the people of the earth may know that the hand of the Lord is mighty"[47] (Joshua 4:24 ESV).

3

CONNECTING THE DOTS

HISTORY WAS ONLY A PASSING interest to me in school until a world history course covering the Sumerian period through the Roman period caught my eye. That was a time in history when many of the events of both the Old Testament and New Testament were taking place. I wondered if history could shed some light on biblical times and events. It was evident in the Bible that world events had significant "hand of God" moments, where God spoke to world leaders and spiritual leaders alike about what was going to happen in their future. But what did history have to say about these things? Boy, did I strike gold! World politics, ancient economics, competition for natural resources; cultural conflict, disparate social paradigms, competing religions; changing climate, changing demographics, and advances in ancient technology taken together overlay the times, places, and people of the Bible, providing context and understanding to many of the events mentioned or referred to in scripture. Grasping Old and New Testament history gave me a broader understanding of how God works with societies, cultures, and nations.

Why did God speak to Jonah and ask him to go to Nineveh as a street preacher when they were a hated enemy? The answer would be found in history more than one hundred years into their future. What drove King David to the roof of his palace only to fall to temptation watching Bathsheba bathe on a neighboring rooftop? It would be decades before the political intrigue neither David nor Bathsheba were aware of would become apparent. What pushed Rome to focus their conquering ambitions on the Middle East? The same few issues that triggered the beginning of the fall of the Roman Empire hundreds of years later. When the sun stood still for Joshua and advanced backward for Hezekiah, was it a miracle or a natural phenomenon? You can see why my excitement over history, especially social history, archaeology, anthropology, geography, meteorology, and geopolitics blossomed! More importantly, the correlation between history and biblical events became clear in a manner that God acting in and through history became transparent. God not only makes himself know to us personally, or through other people, he reveals himself acting through history and the people of the day in significant observable ways. Sometimes it is turning something bad into something good, or protecting persons and even nations from a calamity, or intentionally intervening through natural or miraculous means to keep his plan of redemption on track. And that is a key insight. The Bible is the story of God's plan of redemption for humankind and often will only reference people and events outside of that purpose indirectly or not at all. Even when humanity is at its worst, God will act to keep his plan on track. If we look for it, we will see it like connecting the dots in the sky at night, turning the stars and planets into a recognizable picture. Noticing the themes God is dealing with in the Bible helps us understand what he could be doing in our lives today.

More importantly, what God said and did in history is still unfolding today. The prophet Daniel, in the Old Testament book by his name, after hearing a warning message from God, reveals to King Nebuchadnezzar four world empires, two of them not in existence yet: Assyrian, Babylonian, Persian, and Roman, covering much of the history in the Old Testament and New Testament. Matching history to these time periods helps us understand a lot of actions and events not fully explained in scripture. God breaks through not just throughout our lives but throughout history. Connecting the dots and seeing the big picture reinforces the reality that thin space experiences happen to societies, cultures, cities, and even nations as well as personally to us.

Sometimes this idea of large-scale thin space experiences is difficult to see when just considering scripture without the context of history. One of the reasons these connections can become obscured is clues in the languages used in those times are missed in our English translations. For example, our modern-day word *love* can cover a wide range of meanings, including love of God, love of others, love of self, love of material things; affection, attraction, and desire. There are different words in the original language of the New Testament for each of those nuances. Yet, in our language of today, they can all be translated simply as *love*. Sometimes the context of how the word is used in scripture helps us get the gist of what is intended. It is then that clues to something bigger going on in the background become apparent.

For example, in the well-known Sermon on the Mount, Jesus publicly makes a strong point about authentic lifestyle.[48]

What is clear to us about what he says is that people can be hypocrites when they pretend to be something they are not in order to be noticed by others for their good deeds. But there is so much more beyond this observation to grasp! What is really being addressed is our vanity and our need to be seen by others that pulls us into seeking attention by pretending to be something we are not. The context of a single word can illuminate what we may miss by not going deeper. Imagine this kind of illumination applied on a larger scale and what we might discover!

Back up now and look at a bigger picture. The Pharisees, Sadducees, and Herodians were the three political parties, so to speak, in Israel at the time. Each had to curry favor from the Roman occupiers while competing with one another for control of everything going on in Israel. Culturally, pretending to be something you were not was an approved strategy in life and work. Pretending to be righteous, good, and better than others was one way to secure approval and was a norm for leaders. Not a great example for the people though! The admonition Jesus offers is the recognition you receive from a motive to find approval is all you are going to get. In fact, the particular word used here goes further to including the idea that the one desiring to being the center of attention will miss out on the blessing of God in other ways as well. Wow! That comes across more strongly now that we have a cultural and historical context!

This idea of being seen by others is linked by Jesus to being hypocrites, using a word that comes out of the theater of the day and means to wear a mask hiding your true identity. Theater actors of the day held up masks over their faces to play different parts in the play. Instead, Jesus encourages us not to pretend and not be show-offs even when we have done something praise worthy. It is enough that we keep some things close to our hearts and known only to a few in our circle, and not boast of these things even when the time comes for the world to know. The deeper lesson Jesus is teaching here is that we need to beware of self-glorifying religion. Sometimes God asks us to keep our thin space experiences private or known to only a few so that we are not tempted to use them as a way of getting attention.

Understanding context will make deeper lessons clear, and in that deepening of understanding, we begin to see the handiwork of God on a larger scale. It is not difficult with all the aids we have today to look behind scripture at the history, culture, language, and politics of the times. The deeper you go, the bigger and better the context, and the better to connect the dots and see God working on a mind-blowing scale.

When it comes to the experiences we have with God subtly or dramatically showing up in our lives, the lesson is simple: do not brag about your experiences. Mary, the mother of Jesus, is a great example of holding things close to her heart for only a few to recognize or know about.[49] An angel had appeared to Mary with news of her favor with God and her forthcoming child, the Messiah. Joseph was given a dream featuring an angel with a message of encouragement regarding Mary's pregnancy. Pretty amazing! But both kept these things pretty much to themselves and waited for the time when God would make this news evident, or let them know when it was time to tell others more broadly. Talk about a thin space and God showing up with a clear message!

Here is another cautionary note. Sometimes our memory can play tricks on us.[50] That is one reason why Nancy and I journal in order to get our feelings and facts down when they are fresh. Even in writing this book, we have gone back to each other as well as friends who were part of our experiences together with us. Do they recall these experiences the same way we do? We also confer with scripture, looking for examples and instructions that may apply to thin spaces and whispers.

Recalling memories involves a number of structures in the brain that work together through an organic switchboard to produce a recollection. Sometimes, when we cannot consciously recall everything about a situation, our minds will pull a related memory from somewhere else and drop it in the space where something is missing. This is because our minds crave congruity and consistency and don't like missing pieces of the puzzle. Sometimes our recollections are based upon perceptions that we recall as facts. My perception, say, of an argument I had with my boss may be very different from their perception of that argument, and both of us may disagree with a third party who was a witness to the argument. There are always at least three sides to a story: mine, theirs, and what really happened. It is also natural for us to have more difficulty remembering very difficult or hurtful experiences than remembering positive experiences. We all can identify with conversations about the good old days, recognizing those reminisces come to us far easier than thinking through the painful experiences of those same days. Good and bad experiences go to different places in our brain, and our mind protects us by sheltering us from painful memories so they are not as easy to retrieve. Sometimes while we sleep and dream, we are restructuring memories responding to motivation and desires reflected in our expectations to "get it right" or resolve confusion in an attempt to interpret the world around us. Then, there are also memories that will be crystal clear. The caution is to not assume every recollection we have is reliable but to question, contemplate, and look for ways to understand more clearly or even validate memory and when possible write it down.

Some people can have real difficulty seeing God's handiwork in their lives or being convinced that other people actually have these experiences. Their incredulity may be a result of a habitually negative perspective. When we are constantly negative, critical of others, or persistently sarcastic, we actually blind ourselves to those experiences that push us out of our comfort zone toward a more positive mindset and optimism. This resistance to change comes with a cost. We can become comfortable in our Christianity and not want to change. Jesus ran into this resistance often in his ministry. The cautionary note is to be careful we are not limiting the work of God in our lives by having a critical spirit or a negative attitude.

The Centurion who walked up to Jesus and asked him to cure his servant at home with just a word was open and accepting of the possibility of a miracle.[51] Jesus openly marveled at his faith. The people surrounding them hearing this conversation were comfortable in their traditional beliefs and unwilling to be open to possibilities. We learn more about Jesus's response to this kind of resistance when later he returns to Capernaum. Upon arrival, some people brought a paralytic to him to be healed. Jesus, seeing their faith, told the man his sins were forgiven.[52] Some of the religious leaders, the naysayers of the day who had already established a pattern of criticism trying to tear him down, were scandalized! In those days, it was believed pretty much by everyone that illness was due to sin, and proof of repentance and forgiveness of sin was the actual healing from the illness.

So Jesus tells the man to pick up his bed and go home, and the man did just that to the amazement of the crowd. The crowd rejoiced and gave God the glory! They were open to change, while the naysayers went away probably convinced they had somehow been tricked. For the others, the outward healing and proof of forgiveness could not be denied, and they went away with renewed optimism. Now, we know today that sin and illness do not go hand in hand. But this was the proof his audience in that time and place were looking for. Proof is always available if you look for it. But many will only want to criticize or disprove what they may have just heard or witnessed because it calls them out of where they are in their faith and invites them into a more positive relationship with the Savior.

This concept of God calling us out of where we are and inviting us into a more positive or fruitful relationship with him is integral to hearing from the Holy Spirit and progressing in our journey of faith. God often moves us to a new place by speaking to us. When we understand that our relationship with the Holy Spirit and hearing from him is a part of how we grow and mature in our spiritual walk, we connect the dots to this whole concept of hearing from God through the Holy Spirit and moving forward in our personal spiritual journey. God is continually drawing us to himself or moving us forward in our walk with him. He teaches, shows, speaks, and guides us in many beautiful ways. During this journey, God desires for us a deeper walk with him. Sometimes our spiritual journey with God includes warnings. When God wants to takes us from one place to another, he often provides a cautionary note.

Jeremiah was a prophet who delivered many messages to the Israelites, and he delivered a number of cautionary notes from God as well. The Israelites were worshiping many idols or other gods than the one true God. God asked Jeremiah to warn them: if they continued to worship idols and not acknowledge God as the one true God, there would be consequences to their disobedience. God loved them and wanted a deeper, more intimate relationship. To this end, God's desire was for the situation with Babylon, an emerging world power, and the very real threat of the destruction of Jerusalem and exile to Babylon to draw them back to a vibrant relationship with him. He used a cautionary note or hard situation so they would cry out to him and thus gain the opportunity to return to a right relationship.

The Israelites were rebelling against God and not listening to him and following his ways.

God has great plans for them and knew it was for their best to listen and follow his ways. We often get so focused on pursuing what we desire that we leave God out of our lives. When this happens, God gives us a cautionary note or gets our attention to get us back on track. The warning from Jeremiah is that disobedience has consequences, and obedience brings blessings. God makes it clear all his ways and plans are for our best and will bring hope to our future. Relying on God's knowledge and power requires surrendering to his ways, and when we do surrender and trust him, he will bless us. This is a promise from God! As we look not to the things of this world but to his ways, we can expect a life of adventure for our good.[53] When God wants to take us higher, he first takes us deeper.

As God is taking us deeper in our walk with him, he will often speak to us in ways that challenge us to unpack certain concepts he is teaching us. As a couple, we often hear a similar word from the Holy Spirit and bring a new thought to the other so we can discuss, study, research, and dig deeper into what God is teaching us. This unpacking of a concept requires us to pull out commentaries and Bible dictionaries and look deeper into a subject matter in prayerful consideration. God may not do this with you, but this is how he works in our lives.

During one of our conversations, we realized God was teaching us about how his ways may overlap or overshadow another one of his ways. He was teaching us that even though he may address something, such as honoring the Sabbath, at another time he may ask us to put aside our understanding of the Sabbath in order to give another of his ways a more important place. In this particular case, it was loving a neighbor over honoring the Sabbath. There is no law against doing good for someone at any time. God wanted us to not try to control a situation but to honor him by loving our neighbor.

There is a point to be made here related to the Holy Spirit's role in our relationship with Christ and the caution we must exercise in viewing our experiences with God through the lens of scripture and not just our feelings or religious culture. Sometimes it is easy to "proof text" a biblical principle by isolating it from its context or from other related scripture that applies. It is easy to lose sight of the principle of "scripture informing scripture." The truth in application we may be looking for may not be contained in a single verse but in the balance of several principles. The truth we need in some situations will be the sum of truths or principles we find within a number of related passages. In the example of the Sabbath taken from Matthew 12:1–9 (NIV), Jesus is confronted by the religious experts regarding what is prohibited on the Sabbath. Allowing the disciples to glean grain as well as healing someone on the Sabbath is considered work and prohibited. Jesus reminds them the matter is not so simple, directing them to scriptures that speak clearly to exceptions to be made. Several things his opponents must now consider include the idea that the Law they revere so much was intended to instruct, protect, and guide people and not to hurt them; this Law makes provision for doing good for others and even their livestock never wrong; and they would do well to consider the whole counsel of the Law.

Bottom line, God is helping us connect the dots between his purposes and his loving will for us. Getting ourselves out of the way so this can happen easily means some cautions are in order. Otherwise, we risk creating a formulaic approach to knowing and experiencing God, which can be more representative of our thinking and feeling than his design and purpose for our lives.

This is important to understand when it comes to hearing a word from God and seeing it come to fulfillment. God often speaks something to our heart, and we do not see it come to fruition for years. Think of Abraham and Sarah and the promise of Isaac.[54] Biblical history tells us that from the time the word was spoken from God to Abraham to Sarah becoming pregnant was over ten years![55] Abraham and Sarah waited over ten years to see the fulfillment of the promise of Isaac. You, too, may have to wait many years for the fulfillment of a promise. Some years ago, we were waiting on an impending move and asking God when it would happen when I (Nancy) believed I heard "July." I rushed downstairs to tell Jeff what I believed I heard and shared with him "July." Jeff immediately asked, "Which July?" I gasped, not knowing the answer, and said, "I did not ask God!" The fulfillment of this particular July arrived two years later. Subsequently, God has shown us many lessons throughout the years in July. We laugh together as we see the fulfillment of God's promises can continue to unfold, and we need to be very careful not to put human filters on what God speaks. God's love will make his promises known to us as we continue to seek him and pursue him with a pure heart. Be patient and let a promise you have heard come to fulfillment at the right time. This in itself is a thin space as God reveals his ways and we wait for his timetable to unfold.

There is no one formula for hearing God speak and understanding a thin space. God can touch our lives and his work on this earth in so many ways. His ways often involve many people so his grand purposes are achieved. Let me share one such story that included many thin spaces and many people experiencing thin spaces over many years, which only became understood by all of us after God connected the dots.

Nesoah is a pediatric orthopedic surgeon passionate about serving God, loving people, and helping see children and people of all ages living to their greatest potential. He plays a significant role in inspiring people to lead a life of healing, health, and restoration. He met my (Nancy) brother-in-law, John, many years ago in Cameroon, Africa. John serves the African country of Cameroon with Health Teams International as a medical professional, as an endodontist tending to their dental needs. The entire country has many more demands than the medical teams in the country there can handle. John also trains many other dentists in more advanced techniques. My sister Cindy has traveled with John on many trips to Cameroon, assisting the medical team meet these many demands. It was on one such medical trip that John and Cindy met Nesoah and deepened this profound friendship. They served and ministered to many family medical needs together and developed a very strong friendship over many years.

A few years ago, when Cameroon was in the middle of a civil war threatening doctors, pastors, and humanitarian service workers, it became apparent Nesoah and his family were no longer safe working at a local hospital. A pastor friend of John and Cindy serving in Cameroon had already been evacuated due to numerous threats on his life and violence against church staff. This was the setting when we got a call from John and Cindy asking if we could help safely connect Nesoah to new work in another African country. So Jeff and I contacted our connections in the medical community. CURE International was one such contact. We introduced Nesoah to the senior leadership at CURE in charge of key medical surgeon roles throughout Africa. After an exhausting interview process between Nesoah and CURE, he was offered an orthopedic surgeon position in Niger, hundreds of miles away from Cameroon. Getting there was nearly impossible. Sometimes their journey met dead ends. Sometimes very real danger was involved as they passed through regions of conflict and violence.

It took many more details, communications, and countless document approvals to get Nesoah and his family safely to his new assignment. God raised up the people needed along the way to connect all the dots for this family's safety and purposeful, godly work. This involved many people, some of them total strangers, over many days to provide shelter, food, and transportation across borders. Often Nesoah and his family didn't know how the day would end. We can't even count all the people involved in God's plan in bringing Nesoah and his family to safety and purposeful work that made his heart sing.

The thin spaces in this story are too numerous to count. Truly, looking back and seeing God's hand in this story builds our faith. The emotion evoked is deep, rare, and inspiring. All involved in their part of Nesoah's story recount the details often because it is one that is both miraculous and encouraging since God allowed us to have a role and to see the bigger picture. Our faith has been strengthened, and hope brought light to a dark place!

Being able to listen to the whispers or leading of the Holy Spirit is a gift. You may recall the Day of Pentecost was a day in history when the Holy Spirit came down on many people at one time. After Jesus's resurrection, he said, "It is better that I go away from you and leave the Holy Spirit, the Advocate." The gift of the Holy Spirit allows us to have God's Spirit living inside us, guiding us daily and prompting us to fulfill our God-given purposes. The Holy Spirit is our Advocate, the Helper, the Comforter, whose job is to speak to us and guide us on our spiritual journey. Without the Holy Spirit working in us, we would likely never connect the dots on our own.

4

LISTENING TO THE WHISPERS

WE MET AS ARRANGED IN the Denver airport after traveling from a number of cities across the country. The four of us were sharing a rental car and traveling to a mountain retreat in the Rockies to join another twenty men for a gathering focused on transitions. These men were all leaders in ministry, church, and business, sharing in common three characteristics. We were all nonprofit ministry executives, senior pastors, or business owners; we were all at a transition point in life and work, anticipating a pivot in our careers; and we all were uncertain about the future. This was a confidential meeting including some well-known people who had agreed to a two-year journey that began upon arrival. We all knew someone in the larger group, but no one knew everyone. Now we were planning to spend a week together sharing common experiences, our faith challenges, aspirations for the future, our confusion and doubts, seeking God for direction.

My emotional baggage walking into this experience included conflicting priorities involving family and ministry; a desire to shift the focus of our business to better support our international ministry; and at the same time a need to scale back in this season of life while still fulfilling our purpose and calling. Needless to say, this had been an ongoing conversation for us over the past year, as well as a source of frustration. What do we continue to do, what needs to change, and what do we need to stop doing? It is not as easy as it sounds. Each of these categories impacts relationships, has financial implications, and involves divestiture of not only assets but of longstanding commitments to boards, institutions, and some freedoms. Within a few days, the nature of the retreat and its emphasis of seeking God in a community of seekers looking for some of the same answers made two choices and their implications very clear to me. At this point, I demurred, not wanting to come down on either side of the fence I was sitting on.

Our group was assigned a cabin we called home when not gathering in the lodge or wandering around in the wilderness. The wandering was probably more in my head than in my feet on the ground. However, the long, beautiful vistas and babbling creeks were good for quiet and thoughtful talks with God. Later in the week, after checking in with Nancy and processing some of what we were both experiencing, I turned in early for the night. We all had separate rooms and got along well, checking in with each other at the end of each day. In the middle of the night, I was awakened by a loud noise.

Unsure of what I had heard and raising my head, I turned on a light and looked around the room. No one was there, and nothing had fallen to the floor. Turning out the light, I rolled over, and just as my head hit the pillow, I heard a voice in my ear, so close I could feel their breath as they asked, "What are you going to do?" I was totally freaked out!

Throwing off the covers, I turned the light back on and jumped out of bed. The room was empty, there was not enough room under the bed to hide, and there was no closet. Going to the door, I opened and listened for someone in the hallway. I actually went across the hall and cracked open my neighbor's door. They were snoring. Going downstairs, same story; besides, no one had enough time to avoid discovery, especially since you could not walk anywhere without floorboards creaking loudly.

Returning to my room, I sat on the bed with the light still on, waiting for the adrenalin to flush out of my system. The loud noise was clearly intended to wake me enough so I could not dismiss the message as a dream. And the question, "What are you going to do?" was clearly intended to move me off the fence one way or the other. The question was not "What are you going to choose?" nor was it intended to tell me what to do. It was intended to get me unstuck because, I realized, I already knew what to do in obedience to my merciful, loving Savior who never intends harm for me and always only has my best interests at heart. I just didn't want to embrace the change involved. So I made a choice and slept soundly through the rest of the night. We will revisit my choice of what to do in a moment.

Over the last few days at the retreat, the Holy Spirit began to unpack what next steps needed to be taken and what the shifts would be in order to pivot our life, work, and ministry toward God's exciting plan for the next season of our lives. This began a conversation with Nancy that seamlessly wove together what God had been saying to her during my time away like puzzle pieces coming together. When you are willingly desiring to follow God, he makes it clear and easy to do so.[56] And the breakthrough began with a whisper.

A whisper, as defined in the introduction, is nothing mystical. It is a great word picture of how the Holy Spirit often gets our attention. Speaking very softly, using one's breath without one's vocal cords, is a whisper. Whispers of the heart can be emotions that speak without words to you, conveying feelings of affection, happiness, contentment; loneliness, caution, or worry. Whispers in nature can be the soughing of the wind through the trees, the dripping of water after a rain shower, the sound of waves lapping the shore in the distance. Whispers of memory can bring a fondness to our thoughts as easily as sadness. The Holy Spirit can use all of these whispers to convey a message.

How do we set the stage for listening to whispers and differentiating them from other sounds and impressions in our life? Psalm 119:105 (ESV) describes a time and place where innovation was key to a shepherd's life and work in such a way that it became a great illustration of how God's Word operates in our lives to sharpen our senses. When the flocks of sheep were taken to higher elevations to escape the heat and find good grazing, they would bed down at night in enclosures made of stone or briars. The shepherds would gather nearby for a meal, having to walk the distance in the dark, where there were many opportunities to stumble off the trail. Many methods of lighting their way were developed and included torches, special lamps, and even sandals with a candle somehow affixed in front of the toes. The idea was to provide light immediately where the shepherd was about to place their foot as well as lighting the path ahead. The light would bring out of the darkness anything hidden that might pose a problem.

In the same way, the Word of God reveals to us lessons we would not see and understand were it not for the light of scripture revealing them to us: "Your word is a lamp unto my feet and a light to my path"[57] (Psalm 119:105 ESV). If we are in the Word consistently, even daily, we will have our senses trained to discern things not easily discerned otherwise. The practice of Bible reading, daily devotions, Bible study, scripture memory, praying scripture, and listening to sermons keeps us tuned in and sensitive to what the Holy Spirit has to say. These habits set the stage for us to hear the whispers and know if they are real.

Elijah had an encounter with God where a whisper got his attention, enough for him to actually pay attention to what God literally had to say.[58] The word *whisper* used is compound, combining two ideas representing the idea of a soft, gentle blowing and a hushed whisper. Which was it? Elijah was curious enough to go to the entrance of his hiding place and actually hear God's voice. This idea of using a whisper to get someone's attention before speaking to them was a common practice, and we find another example in the conversation Eliphaz has with Job, though here it is an ordinary conversation between friends.[59] It is the same thing we would do when we were children, when we would say softly, "Pssst! Pssst!" to someone to draw them aside and have a private conversation. Whispers may be a clear message or something designed to get our attention. Well, it certainly got my attention, and the message was very clear!

Some people are disinclined to believe in the supernatural. I am inclined to think these occurrences are natural when they are genuine and are a reflection of God's desire to have a relationship with us that communicates to us in ways that fit who we are. Not everyone has these experiences as often as other people seem to have them. Perhaps they don't need the reassurance that God is here now as much as I do. Or it may be something that is altogether outside of their experience and sphere of thought.

We all have boundaries to our thinking that are formed by our enculturation, socialization, education, and life experience. When we are confronted with something that exceeds these boundaries, we are skeptical and can easily dismiss someone else's understanding or conviction about these kind of things. This is bounded-set thinking. Our boundaries bind us up to possibilities ... *I can't believe it because it is beyond my experience.* Boundaries are good. However, when we are seeking to know the truth, we may need to step outside of our usual sphere of thought and be more centered-set in our thinking. This doesn't mean we become open to anything or set discernment and wisdom aside. Remember, boundaries are good. Centered-set thinking focuses on one thing, in this case the truth about these kind of experiences. How do you satisfy yourself that these things really can happen to people? By investigating with an open mind not hampered by stereotypes or prejudices.

Honest doubt is a good thing and should propel us into a search for truth. However, if we are reluctant to find truth, we may sabotage our efforts. Beware of a superficial experience with your own divine moment. If you earnestly seek God, you will find him.[60] If you are timid or superficial, you are likely to only find more questions.

A number of years ago, I (Nancy) during my quiet time sensed God was encouraging me to loosen my grip on a number of people and places and instead "grip my ways, my direction." Writing these exact words down in my journal proved to be very helpful because they did not completely make sense at the time. I sensed God identified three important places I was to "loosen my grip" on so I could then lay hold of the new God had for me. Sometimes God gives us a message that not only informs us but creates a sense of awareness that has us looking for what comes next. I would revisit what I needed to loosen my grip on as I prayed and surrendered to God. Then approximately four years later, I sensed God saying you have to "let go" to "grab ahold" of the new. "Grab ahold of my (God's) ways, my direction, and my gifts for you." He is doing something new. It appeared God was bringing me back around to this same subject, yet I did not know where he was going with it. Some of it was clear, yet the entire message was not completely clear. So I prayed, tested, and searched for discernment. Jeff and I discussed these challenges; we prayed, tested, checked, and searched for discernment together. There was a significant amount of waiting during this time of praying, testing, and seeking understanding. At one point, we actually thought it meant one outcome and with a slammed door realized that was not the answer.

Recently, God unfolded more of the picture. It became clear what he was asking us to loosen our grip on and what we should grip moving forward. He was clearly doing a new thing as in Isaiah.[61] It was not an easy process, yet the clarity that came made the outcome clear to us, and God kept confirming the answer to both Jeff and me individually and together. Sometimes God does not reveal or unpack the meaning of what he has said until many years later. In the middle of this revelation, we can experience a time of waiting for him to reveal more of the detail and how it applies to us. At one point, I wrote in my journal that I had a frustrating lack of passion about letting go of the things God was asking me to let go. We continued to see there were many areas we needed to "let go" so we could "grab ahold" of the new." One of the aspects we were letting go of was California as we considered a significant move to Arizona. We enjoyed many trips there in the past, we have family who lives there, our daughter used to live there, and our twin grandchildren were born there. Yet leaving what we loved in California—people, ministry, the beach, and a climate that felt like home because it was home—was harder to surrender and completely let go.

In Matthew 11:1–6 (ESV), Jesus is instructing the disciples when they received word from John the Baptist asking, "Are you the one who is to come or shall we look for another?" Jesus said,

"Go and tell John what you hear and see: the blind received their sight and the lame walk, lepers are cleansed and the deaf hear, and the dead are raised up and the poor have good news preached to them. And blessed is the one who is not offended by me."[62] This is quite a profound answer to John's question, and I believe it applies to us here. Jesus asked John the Baptist to look closely at the evidence Jesus was providing. When you see God moving, test, check, discern, pray, see, and do not be offended by what God is doing in your life. Grab ahold of it; grab ahold of the new. You will see the evidence just as John the Baptist did. God wants to be understood, and it will be there to be seen.

Dreams and visions are like whispers when it comes to getting our attention and delivering a message. But not every dream is a message from God, and visions can be nothing more than imaginative daydreams. How do we tell the difference?

Dreams are a natural product of our physiology and psychology, playing a healthy role in our lives.[63] Dreams can be responses to our external environment. For example, a noise heard in the night that does not fully awaken us but requires a rational explanation. Dreams can also be a response to our internal environment: too much pepper on too much pizza that we had for dinner that is now talking back to us with discomfort. Again, it is a physical stimulus for which our mind requires an explanation, using imagination and creativity to produce an answer. Our minds always seek congruity.[64] The mind likes balance, calm, and tranquility, like a pool of undisturbed water reflecting mirrorlike the inherent peace, equilibrium, and stability pictured here. Dreams are also a mechanism for working out solutions while we sleep. How many times have you awakened in the night with an idea, a solution, an answer and turned over and gone back to sleep, telling yourself you will remember it in the morning. The only problem is we usually do not remember! This is one reason why I keep a notepad on the night table beside the bed. Stress is usually the culprit when this happens, but stress can get out of hand. It depends on what your subconscious mind is trying to resolve.

Often, our subconscious mind shifts into problem-solving mode while we sleep but is missing a few pieces of the puzzle. When we sleep, problem-solving can be more difficult than when in awake states because working memory (where conscious thought occurs) must access short-term and long-term memory, as well as other functions in our brain that may be offline. When there is a mix-up, our mind will borrow a bit of recollection from something else and slip it into the empty spot it is trying to fill.[65] This can create some very interesting associations in our dreams. This hiccup in trying to rationalize our thoughts while sleeping happens, because our brains work differently, in some respects, while we are asleep. Some functions in our brain go into their own sleep mode, like our computers do when we do not want to shut them down entirely, and are not available.

For example, while we sleep and dream, our brains are working without the benefit of our logic filter. This can certainly make for some spectacular dreams. Recently, I had a dream where I was piloting a jet fighter. Ready for takeoff at the end of the runway, I was cleared for departure. It was a very vivid and realistic dream. I could hear the engines spool up, feel the uneven thumping of the landing gear as the aircraft began to gain speed down the runway, and see the nose lifting as I pulled back on the stick and the runway fell away below. And then I crashed. My wife was awakened by my hand and leg motions, and when I leapt out of the bed, diving up into the air only to crash to the floor, hitting my head on the side table, she panicked. To make matters worse, I was awake then, leaning back against the bed, laughing aloud as I realized what happened. She thought I had lost my mind. Dreams can be very realistic and very persuasive to the dreamer.

However, the Holy Spirit does not give us nightmares; nor does he instruct us to do something against what we find in the Bible as expectations for right living. Is your dream coherent? Does it make sense to you? Were you free from feelings of anxiety, fear, or harm when experiencing your dream? Visions can be even more complexing since daydreaming can produce some pretty vivid images while you are wide awake and drifting off, say for example, from a boring sermon.

During a particularly difficult season in church ministry characterized by a great deal of spiritual warfare, I became increasingly concerned and worried about how Nancy was holding up under all the pressure. Sitting in church one Sunday morning during this time, thinking about the situation and reaching out to God in the few moments before getting up to preach, I noticed a bright light off to my left. Looking up, I saw myself with Nancy on my left, standing in the area between the front row where I was physically seated and the stage where the pulpit stood waiting. Next to Nancy on her left was a huge angel dressed in brilliant white (no wings or halos, just clothes suitable for church). He was so tall his right hand rested naturally on her left shoulder. He had to be ten or twelve feet tall! A voice impressed me with a message, "Don't worry about Nancy. I have got her in my hand." What an encouraging message! Use dreams and visions to inform you and alert you, and ask God for clarification. Do not try to make more out of them than is there to see.

Earlier, we told the story of Elijah hearing God speak through a whisper, a still, small voice. Elijah repeated, "I have been very zealous for the Lord God," coming off the miracle where God miraculously showed up in the fire, proving he is the only true God. Yet now Elijah is fearful and running for his life from Queen Jezebel, who wants to kill him. Elijah is exhausted, fearful, and feeling lonely, and many historians and commentaries agree Elijah is probably depressed because of the situation. God comforts Elijah in the kindest way by sending an angel of the Lord to deliver water and baked bread over hot coals, along with a message of encouragement and presence. The angel of the Lord says to Elijah, "Get up and eat, for the journey is too much for you."[66] God deals gently with Elijah because he knows what he has just been through. Even though it was profoundly victorious, it was stressful, and now running for his life placed stress upon stress. So God takes him through a process to restore him and patiently prepare him for what is next. Take some time and read this whole story in 1 Kings 19, as it is one of the most moving stories of restoration in the Old Testament. This vision Elijah has seen is a beautiful story of God's tender mercy!

Like the story of Elijah, sometimes it can be difficult to determine if what we experience is a vision or an actual experience of God's physical presence, or both. Abraham and Sarah as well as the apostle Peter had experiences that had elements of all three situations.

Abraham and Sarah are another example of God showing up in their lives to prepare them for what was ahead. Both had a profound interaction with God, which is recorded in Genesis 18. Abraham was approximately ninety-nine years old, and Sarah was probably eighty-nine years old one year before Isaac was born. Imagine God sending "three men"[67] to deliver a message that in your old age, you will be having a son. Most commentators believe two of the men were angels, and the third was the Lord himself. This son will be in the lineage of David and the Messiah to come. Talk about a vision and message that was far from ordinary, containing a message that required significant faith! Faith in the unordinary requires significant belief that God can and will work in ways such as a vision or a dream. God's miraculous hand may challenge you to believe something your friends and neighbors may not have as easy a time believing until it comes to fruition. Your faith will grow and mature as you trust God in these extraordinary situations. To say,

"I believe, help my unbelief," is a prayer you may pray many times as God speaks through visions and dreams.[68]

You may also be familiar with the famous story of Peter in Acts 12:5–17. Peter was in prison, and the church was earnestly praying for Peter, when a light shined in his cell. An angel of the Lord tapped him on his side, woke him up, and removed the chains on him. The angel said, "Quick, get up!" Peter's chains fell off his wrists. The angel said, "Put on your clothes, sandals, and cloak," and let's get out of here. Actually, the angel said, "Follow me," but you get the idea. This account of Peter told by Paul in Acts also indicates Peter does not know at first if this a dream or really happening. We can all relate to a feeling of uncertainty. Yet Peter soon realizes that what is happening to him is real. The angel disappears, and Peter gets ahold of himself and heads to the home of Mary, the mother of John Mark. God just saved Peter and sent him on his way to keep preaching the Gospel. Clearly nothing is too hard for God, and he has a message for Peter to deliver. This story has many lessons wrapped up in it, all showing the great things God can do as well as how he cares and provides for his children. All these stories require an element of wisdom and spiritual eyes given to us by the Holy Spirit. Even though there are the events of the dream or vision, there is always at least one underlying lesson and takeaway God is showing us.[69]

When God uses extraordinary ways to get our attention, it is important to keep in mind the point is the message God wants to deliver, not the signs and wonders. We will explore signs and wonders and their purpose later in the book.

When people describe God as speaking "out loud," they often mean more than a whisper or a spoken voice. Dreams, visions, a touch, a sound, observing what God is doing with keen spiritual insight are also included in the idea of "out loud," in the sense of something that clearly caught our attention in a loud sort of way. God can communicate through all of our senses. Usually this is accomplished in a casual manner, which we may not recognize until after the fact when we are reflecting on the experience. Sometimes it can be dramatic because he wants our attention *now*!

So it was in the case of the whispered question, "What are you going to do?" I understood clearly what God was asking of us, and I did not want to do it! The whisper was not to provide guidance or reveal some spiritual truth. It was a reminder to me that passivity in the face of a clear calling is sin. That was the fence I was riding, and the time had come for me to act, or the timeline simply would pass me by. This whisper and the breath of the spoken word on my ear was like a gunshot in the manner it got my immediate attention. Sometimes God speaks loudly even in a whisper.

Beauty and creativity are God's creation, which he has gifted us in capacity to appreciate and even marvel over. Sometimes simply enjoying a mountain vista, listening to a babbling brook, enjoying nature outdoors releases our tension and energizes us. Creativity in action has the same effect as we give expression to our thoughts and feelings. My creative escape from stress is art, especially in reproducing nature scenes and native animals. Life comes into better focus when we give free expression to the whispers, the messages, that are already built into us from birth. Without the gift of appreciation for beauty and creativity, these messages would be lost.

Music and singing alone or with others is another way to tap into these connections. I love singing contemporary choruses without the music or picking up a hymnal and reading or singing out loud some of the great hymns. Worship in church accompanied by music is a wonderful place to connect with the message. This isn't hocus-pocus. There are good neurological explanations for why this happens. The outcome is what thrills me.

What gets caught up in the mind is freed in the heart when we sing to the Lord. The song is for the singer because underneath the words, there is always a whisper.

5

RECOGNIZING A
THIN SPACE

GOD CAN BREAK THROUGH INTO our lives at any time, even when the foundation is missing for being aware of when this happens. He is God and wants to communicate with us in ways we understand. Most of the time when this occurs, it is in the context of the ongoing relationship we have with him rather than something unusual or surprising out of the blue. One of the results of continuity in this relationship is the expectation of awareness we carry with us throughout the day. We expect an impression, a word, a directed focus, an intuition and are not surprised when it happens. This expectation over time develops a readiness to listen when God does show up, making it much easier to discern when God is breaking through to you.

There was an occasion when Nancy and I were leading a mission trip to Trinidad and Tobago. Just getting the team assembled and at the airport at the same time met with one obstacle after another. Once there, we learned our sponsoring church had left boxes and boxes of materials to take with us no one had planned to carry. We had to obtain duffel bags the airline would accept, check it all in as freight, pay the bill, and get on our plane in time for departure. We all felt some serious resistance happening, and already tempers were getting shorter, and some fingers were pointing at likely targets for this fiasco.

When we arrived very late at night at the Trinidad airport, we discovered the customs agents wanted a huge sum of money for our duffel bags in order to get them into the country. This was a severe problem. However, God had been speaking to all of us in very personal ways before this trip had even gotten underway. Suddenly, I had this sense of peace settle over me, and an idea formed in my mind. I pulled the group to the side with all our luggage and freight and said, "Just wait." *Wait for what?* the team demanded to know! All I could say was, "God is in control, and everything is going to be all right." I had no idea what we were waiting for but did have the expectation of awareness that God was going to do something. After about twenty minutes, another customs agent, this one apparently with senior rank, showed up, conferred with the other agents, and then waved us down to an open lane and checked us and all our stuff in without a problem or a fee.

Evidently, the night supervisor had called in sick, and our agent had been called to take his shift as the night supervisor. Turns out he was also a Christian. God wanted us to wait; help was on the way. This began a trip filled with breakthroughs for all of us day after day.

The importance of listening, of having an expectation of awareness, cannot be underestimated. The Israelites had a difficult time learning this lesson in the period of Judges when everyone did what was right in their own eyes. Midian, a neighbor located southeast of Israel, took advantage of Israel's lack of leadership during this period and would sweep in each year at harvest time and steal all the food and livestock they could, leaving the Israelites hungry and hiding in caves.[70]

God makes it clear throughout the book of Judges that sin, beginning with not listening to God, can cause loss of everything important to them. The book reveals a persistent pattern over more than three hundred years of rebellion, growing decline leading to exposure and invasion by their enemies, repentance, and restoration following acknowledgment of God and his promises.

Matthew (NIV) describes the exact opposite of rebelling against God's ways when he tells the parable of a man who, after finding a hidden treasure in a field, went and sold all he had to buy the field.[71] This is an illustration of men and women who find their relationship with God so joyful and important they will sell everything they have to follow God. When the kingdom of heaven is our greatest treasure, we will put aside worldly possessions and worldly desires to follow God and his ways. This requires hearing from God regarding what he may be asking us to personally loosen our grip on in order to follow his direction for us. Clearly not everyone is asked to sacrifice and sell everything to follow God. It is especially important to hear from God what he specifically wants us to give up, do, leave, or sell in order to buy into what he has for us. Living a sold-out life for God comes at a cost of letting go of worldly ways to grab ahold of what God has for us. Counting the cost of following Jesus is an important subject. When you find something of great value, you will do anything to obtain it. This is what God desires of us. To loosen our grip on the world and to grab ahold of what he has for us as citizens of the kingdom of heaven. Our relationship with God is our greatest joy. It is our greatest treasure.

As we mentioned in the introduction, when God breaks through into our lives and we have a personal encounter with God, our role is to follow his lead. To listen and do what God says is a profound part of our walk with God. Whether it is a simple instruction, word of encouragement, or an ask with high stakes requiring much faith. All these encounters with God are a part of our relationship with God and spiritual journey, which is why it is so important to listen.

There is a rub to all of this, a frustrating dichotomy that makes us wonder if God did really break through to us. This is the boundary layer between sanctified intuition and imagination. Intuition and imagination are closely related, even to the point of sharing some of the same structures in our brain. It is no wonder that at times we cannot tell which is which!

Imagination is the ability to be creative or resourceful, forming ideas, images, and concepts with originality. Imagination helps us examine and test things as well. How often have you said to yourself, "What if ..." and proceeded to evaluate the possibilities of an idea? When we recall memories that include sights and sounds as well as feelings associated with that memory, we are using imagination.

The parts of the brain involved in imagination are the neocortex at the back of the brain, the thalamus located between the left and right hemispheres of the brain, and the posterior precuneus.[72] These structures are also involved in vision and recreating visual images, consciousness and alertness, and abstract thinking. Some of these structures are also used in our instinctive responses or intuition. This is one reason we sometimes stop and ask ourselves, "Am I imagining things, or is this gut feeling I have something to pay attention to?"

Intuition is an ability to understand or know something without any apparent thought process involved. This impression of correctness in the absence of conscious reasoning sometimes leads to questioning our own thinking. The right side of our brain is the center for nonverbal, intuitive, holistic modes of thinking, while the left side of our brain is where language and logic dominate. In fact, intuition operates throughout the entire right side of our brain as well as the hippocampus, our gut, and the enteric nervous system (the nervous system of the gut).[73]

The left and right hemispheres of our brains inform each other. Intuition draws on data and deep memory and processes these in the right hemisphere in response to subconscious pattern recognition. When this happens, our body starts firing neurochemicals in our brain and our gut, communicating with each other. This is where the expression "gut feeling" comes from. An actual sensation can be produced in our stomach and intestines. The part of the brain that fires up the most when this happens is the precuneus, which is also fired up when imagination is at work. It is easy to understand why it is difficult at times to discern if what you sense is a product of your imagination, or intuition, or just wishful thinking. Wishful thinking can be a filter that causes bias in our imagination and intuition.

The best thing to do is to give it time to sort itself out. Pray for discernment. Wait and give it a little more time. Pray for God to reveal the truth behind what confuses or concerns you. Find a trusted adviser when the time is right to share what you are looking for discernment regarding. Ask them to pray with you. Be patient and let God reveal the truth. God often reveals something many years in advance to prepare us for something. Yet sometimes our brain does not separate imagination from intuition, and we may have to live with no answer for some time.

We are more than just our biology, and we need to give our biology time to settle down so our thinking can be influenced by conscious thought and the Holy Spirit. Uncertainty and confusion will relent, and a clearer, conscious understanding will emerge.

Confusion can be a part of our lives from time to time in an enduring manner. Often this is due to our health. Mental wellness is thinking, feeling, and acting in ways that create healthy physical and social well-being. Your mind is in order and functioning in your best interest. Healthy body leads to healthy brain and is a balance of good nutrition, plenty of exercise, sufficient sleep, meaningful relationships, a sense purpose in life, and continuing spiritual renewal. This balance in life and work leads to greater self-awareness and self-management and an ability to discern when God is about to break through based on intuition, not imagination.

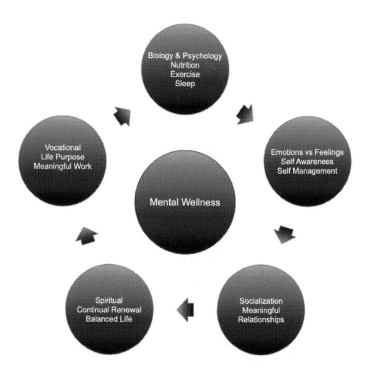

Just a few years ago, Bruce and I were traveling to a former communist country in Eastern Europe to begin a ministry there involving humanitarian medical missions. God had prompted the minister of defense to call Bruce some months earlier, asking for help with an epidemic of suicide. This was still a communist country. We ended up being the first Westerners to teach in their National Medical University as well as their Ministry of Defense in nearly seventy-five years. We were on edge as we traveled, largely because we knew there was strong opposition to our going. We also were uncomfortable with the way this engagement began.

Bruce had been in a taxi traveling from the Kyiv airport in Ukraine to our seminary in the city, where we train chaplains for service in hospitals, prisons, and the military. The taxi driver received a phone call and, after a brief conversation that Bruce did not understand, handed the phone to Bruce, saying, "It's for you," in heavily accented Ukrainian. Bruce answered the phone. It was the minister of defense in a neighboring country asking for help. He wanted Bruce to meet with him on the following Monday. What concerned us was somehow someone knew where Bruce was at that specific time and how to reach him in the taxi on the driver's phone and not Bruce's phone.

On this trip, Bruce and I had been significantly delayed due to an airport shutdown en route. The resulting logjam of travelers was overwhelming, and we were sure we would miss the last flight to our destination. My heart sank. We stood there looking up at the flight schedule board, confused, when a sense of calm just settled over me. I questioned for a moment if I was imagining things, or intuitively did I sense God was going to show up? At that moment, a woman in an airline uniform we did not recognize walked up to us and asked us to follow her. She led us to the diplomat gate and, in spite of our telling her we were not diplomats, ushered us through the gate and to our aircraft.

When we arrived at our destination, we asked if our host had arranged this privilege. They denied any knowledge of or involvement in what happened. Passing back through the same airport on the way home, we asked about the uniformed lady who picked us out in the middle of a thousand stranded travelers. No one was aware of such a service, and the uniform we described was not used by any airline or airport personnel. I thought back to other times when I needed to be reminded of my own words, "God is in control, and everything is going to be all right." To this day, I am thankful Bruce and I stopped and just stood there long enough for intuition to override imagination.

In Acts chapter 17 (ESV), Paul uses the Bereans as an illustration of a group of people who do not just listen and learn from Paul. They go home, read the scriptures, and research for themselves if what Paul is saying aligns with scripture and what the Holy Spirit is teaching them. Paul does not outline the entire process; he just says, "They received the word with all eagerness, examining the Scriptures daily to see if these things were so"[74] (Acts 17:11 ESV). What Paul is saying is go settle it in your heart as well. Do not take everything at face value. This requires discipline and an eagerness to study, learn, and examine. It takes further insight to test, pray, and listen to God for further insight. We probably do not do this enough in most situations. Jeff and I need to remind each other often to make sure we are pondering, waiting, testing, and examining a certain situation. We are looking for confirmation or a validation of what we believe or think is truth.

An illustration of a spiritual insight is when Nicodemus finally understood what it meant to be "born again" from a spiritual perspective versus trying to figure out how someone could enter a second time into a mother's womb and be born again.[75] These insights that are truly spiritual in nature are only revealed through the Holy Spirit in our lives. Just understanding a concept is different from truly seeing the spiritual revelation and how it applies to our spiritual journey with Jesus. These spiritual insights are to be acknowledged and appreciated as they, too, are God breaking through everyday situations. The Bible repeatedly reminds us that spiritual insight can only be revealed to us by God the Father.[76] If we are to do anything spiritual or understand a spiritual concept, it must come from the Father. He alone, through the work of the Holy Spirit, can reveal these to us.

So we are "testing the spirits" in order to hear from God what is of him and what is imagination. This often takes time and revelation. Yet sometimes God breaks through in an instant, and we are sure it was God and have no question. One time many years ago, I (Nancy) was in a church service and clearly felt an impression from God that this season was "done." God was finished working in this season, and there would be no more spiritual fruit. The impression of "done" was super clear and not confusing at all. It was not an easy message, yet it was clear, and I knew in an instant what it meant. Jeff and I continued to pray to confirm the Lord's message, yet the message never changed. My heart knew in that moment what the Lord meant and what I was to do. This confidence does not always show up in a breakthrough moment from God. We spoke earlier of God moving us to Arizona, and the thin spaces of God speaking around this move was a process to understand, follow, and be obedient. God took us on an interesting journey as he gave us some advance notice, prepared us, and then revealed when to go and where. It was a very lengthy and complex process.

Testing God's voice and direction in this situation was more complex. At different times in our journey, we must do our best to not jump to conclusions. God is full of mercy and allows us to figure this out over time. He is patient with us as we test, stumble, and sometimes get it right at first, and other times it takes a few attempts to understand his will in a situation. These breakthroughs give us purpose in the moment and reveal a purpose for the future. When God speaks, he has a distinct purpose. It is our role to join in with God's spiritual revelation versus only grasping the immediate physical implications. Like Nicodemus, we begin to grasp the spiritual purpose and message of being born again.

Personally, I (Jeff) am frustrated sometimes why God does not make everything clear from the beginning. Yes, there are physiological reasons why we get confused in our mind at times, but is there more to it than our biology? Yes, there is! Here are several reasons that help us understand the purpose of breakthroughs and why they sometimes can be unfathomable.

Wrestling things out for ourselves is great practice when it comes to growing in our ability to be discerning.[77] If everything were perfectly clear and easily understood, there would be no growth in our ability to be discerning. It is not what I know that trains me; it is what I do with what I know. It is not what I understand that makes me mature but what I put into practice.

Jesus Christ wants to have a relationship with us. We are all familiar with the idea that God pursues us because he loves us. It is also true that we pursue God, and when we seek him, we find him.[78] The Holy Spirit places this curiosity, this desire for relationship, in us, especially when we are looking for answers.[79]

Sometimes our expectations or our filters get in the way of clarity. Life in Christ is a journey that begins with the idea of following Christ. Peter responded literally to this call when Jesus said, "Follow Me and I will make you fishers of men"[80] (Matthew 4:19 NIV). Though our call may be different, the idea behind "follow me," as the word was used with Peter, carries the idea that following means leaving other things behind. Some of us do not want to leave other things behind. Some of us may be willing to if we know in advance what that may mean. What Jesus is looking for is commitment. So important is this idea that Jesus made it clear to a crowd of curious onlookers that if they wanted to know God's will, a prerequisite to understanding his teaching is to be committed to doing God's will. In other words, if we want to know what God wants to reveal to us in advance of any commitment, it might not be revealed to us.[81] Jesus wants us to be committed, not half-hearted, not holding back, not looking for better options when we commit to following him.

The purpose of breakthroughs has everything to do with our relationship with Jesus, our growth in that relationship, and our commitment to follow Jesus.

6

SIGNS, WONDERS,
AND MIRACLES

SOMEONE RAISED GEORGE FROM THE dead.

Miracles can often raise in me strong skepticism and questions. But someone raised George from the dead. He was definitely dead, and then he was alive. My doubt clearly has its roots in my nature, but it also has its roots in my embarrassment. When I was a young, new believer, I ran across a scripture that seemed to promise to grant a first prayer request if you had never asked Jesus for anything previously.[82]

Kind of a "get out of jail free" card. I held on to that idea, waiting for something I really needed. Naive and immature, I know.

A time came when I was away at a conference and a friend called asking for prayer. He was a believer as well but more mature than I was. His daughter had a ruptured appendix and was rushed to the hospital from the urgent care center where she had been taken. At the hospital, they confirmed the diagnosis and prepped her for surgery. They also told my friend that it had taken too long to get her medical attention and that she might die. I told God I was sorry I held out on my prayer coupon for selfish reasons and wanted now to use it for my friend's daughter. Then I prayed for her healing.

When I got to the hospital, I found them in the waiting room. To my surprise, they were waiting for her to be discharged. Evidently, when they put her on the table, the surgeon could find nothing wrong with her. The appendix was healed. The doctor said it was a miracle. I told my friend about my prayer, and he very kindly and gently helped me understand there is no prayer coupon in the Bible. God does answer prayer, but when he perform miracles, if indeed that was what this was, he did it for his glory and his purposes, not for ours.

I believe God answers prayers. In that moment, I was also ashamed and embarrassed by my youthful selfishness and lack of understanding. Realizing in the moment that risking trust can come back to bite you, making it clear to me and others that I was a bozo, I would keep my prayers to myself in the future. Oh, I understood something seemingly miraculous had happened, even though I have no idea to this day what really happened. But I was still making everything in my life about me, and that produced the kind self-protective behavior that is like a veil over our mind, preventing us from seeing proof in the healing, or any miraculous event for that matter.

God delights in our foolishness when it gives him opportunity to demonstrate his presence and love in our lives. Over the years since then, I have had a number of cancer scares that mysteriously disappeared after diagnosis. God has a sense of humor, for sure!

The first time this happened, I was provisionally diagnosed with Hodgkin's disease. When I returned to the hospital for treatment, the suspected cancer was gone. The second occasion was a case of skin cancer that was excised with no problem. The third occasion was a diagnosis of early-stage prostate cancer. When I showed up for my third-month monitoring appointment, the test results were normal. The problem had disappeared.

So were any of these miracles of healing, or were they diagnostic errors that cleared up over time? One might say that removing the skin cancer was a miracle of modern medicine, so to speak, but what about the other two? To this day, I do not have an answer, though my medical background suggests they were diagnostic errors. And that is the challenge of actual miracles: they defy explanation in terms of science. Often our naiveté viewing prayer as a free wish, confusion about what is a miracle and what is not, and lack of relevant knowledge at the time get in the way of seeing God break through life and circumstance in miraculous ways. Now let's get back to George.

George died, and somehow he was raised from the dead.

George was a physical fitness nut. Always exercising at the gym, swimming miles in the open ocean, and especially focused on nutrition, he was a good friend and fellow sailor. Yes, of course he had a sailboat we all enjoyed taking out on sunny days. He was a real outdoorsman, physical fitness kind of guy in the best of health.

Stepping off the treadmill one day at the gym, George passed out and hit his head on the concrete floor, hard enough to hear across the room. An off-duty policemen and an off-duty fireman happened to be in the gym as well and ran to George's aid. George was not breathing and had no discernable pulse. CPR was started immediately, and 911 was called. He still was not breathing by the time the ambulance arrived, and they did not get him breathing on his own until he was halfway to the hospital in the ambulance.

We were told later he was unconscious and not breathing on his own for at least seven minutes, if not more. The outlook was very dim indeed.

His wife joined him at the hospital and was frantic. The hospital wanted to keep him there, but Theresa knew their hospital some miles away was better equipped to handle this sort of injury and asked that George be transferred. The hospital said no, he stays here. Theresa was frantic and began to pray. *What to do? Is it better for George to stay here? Why are they not letting me have my husband transferred?* She was confused and panicked, paralyzed in the moment. She left the ICU to get a breath of fresh air.

During this time, a friend they had not seen in some time was driving home and had the sudden very strong urge to go to the hospital. Someone there needed his help. Steve was a lawyer; how could someone at the hospital need his help? Steve was convinced this was God breaking through, so he went to the hospital. He assumed it was an emergency and probably involving someone in ICU, so he took the elevator to the ICU floor, and when the door opened, there was Theresa standing in the elevator alcove in tears, not knowing what to do. She quickly explained the situation, and Steve the attorney got the details straightened out, and George was transferred. Steve told her she needed to have friends with her and not be alone. That was when Theresa called us. She also told us God had told her in the alcove that George was going to fully recover. He told us the same thing on the drive to the hospital.

A week later, George was brought out of the induced coma used to bring the brain swelling down. They thought it was likely he would not breathe on his own. He did. They thought he would be brain dead. He wasn't. They thought there would be serious neural impairments complicating recovery and that full recovery was not possible. He recovered fully. His neurologist was dumfounded and had no explanation. Nancy and I just prayed.

In fact, a lot of their friends came and laid hands on George lying there covered in tubes, praying for George and Theresa just like we did. The ICU nurse, noticing improvements in George after these prayer visits, began to shoo others away when those praying friends of George and Theresa showed up. She was a firm believer in prayer makes a difference. But that was not the only miracle taking place at the time. Nancy and I would often have to wait in the waiting room for the prayer warriors in his ICU cubicle to leave so we could be next to pray over him.

This went on for several weeks. Word began to get around. In the waiting room, people asked if we were the ones praying for a patient in the ICU. They had been there a number of times seeing their own loved ones in critical condition and asked us to pray for them as well. Well, things began to happen, and word spread further. People in other parts of the hospital, hearing what was happening, were waiting for us in the waiting room to show up for our regular visit … asking for prayer for healing, restoration of relationships, and strengthening of their faith. After a few more days, people from the community with no one in the hospital began showing up, asking for prayer and asking for us to tell them about Jesus Christ. The waiting room felt more like a revival church service than a place of trepidation and sorrow.

George fully recovered and returned to life and work with Theresa by his side. The four of us still go sailing now and then. Was it a miracle of modern medicine, or did God step out of the natural order and raise George from the dead? Considering what George told us about his experience through all of this, and what was happing in the waiting room next door, I would say yes to both. So let's revisit the conversation about signs and wonders and their purpose and then talk about miracles, real miracles that teach us so much about God.

God often desires to get our attention before he delivers a

particular message. The Holy Spirit speaks to us in signs and wonders, using the ordinary to convey the extraordinary. This concept, *signs and wonders*, finds its origin in the Old Testament and was familiar to Jews and non-Jews in the early church.[83] As time went by, the phrase fell out of use and was replaced by more contemporary terms. This is one reason why there is some confusion over what this phrase means and how it was used. The word *sign* in this phrase was a particular word in the language of the New Testament giving attention to or pointing to something. In this case, pointing to a message that may be literal or figurative. The *wonder* in this phrase has a similar affect but is usually intended to illustrate something about the message. Together, they act to draw our attention to something else but are not that something else they point out and illustrate.

In Acts 3:1–26 (ESV), Peter heals a lame beggar.[84] It is not surprising that Luke, the author of Acts, includes this miracle right after mentioning wonders and signs in the previous verses ending chapter 2. What is the sign here? What is the wonder? What is the message? In other words, what is being pointed out, what is being illustrated, and what is the message to the blind beggar, the disciples, and to the crowd of witnesses? Look carefully; it may not be the same message to all of them. It should not be surprising to us that God will use the spectacular at times to get our attention.[85]

George's miraculous story continues to unfold years later as we see new meaning and understanding. A week after George was healing in the rehab ward of the hospital, the doctor who initially treated him showed up to see him personally because he had heard through the nursing staff of George's condition. The doctor could not believe he was recovering, speaking, walking, and coherent. The doctor had to see with his own eyes how George was recovering. That story alone made it around the hospital and among George's friends. Sometimes breaking through into our lives needs to be obvious and unmistakable.

Signs, wonders, and miracles in today's parlance are often taken as meaning the same thing. However, in scripture, signs and wonders can occur in the absence of miracles as well. How are miracles different?

There are many definitions for a miracle. The underlying supposition behind whether miracles are even possible, or if they are natural or supernatural, adds to the confusion. We consider a genuine miracle to be defined as a work wrought by a divine power by means beyond the reach of man.[86] Simple and clear, leaving room for consideration of instrumentality: is it God, man, or both who are involved in the miraculous? Ultimately, God is the one responsible for miracles either way. The conflict some experience with the idea of supernatural miracles is that they defy the laws of nature.

These laws have been discovered and proven to be unchanging. They explain how the universe works but do not explain who designed or caused these laws to exist. Miracles are not a violation of these laws but rather the introduction of something outside the laws of nature. Surely, the creator of the universe can operate outside of these laws in miraculous ways, according to his purpose and will. Miracles are a form of revelation, providing authentication that there is a God. The laws of nature define how the universe works, not who God is. Even though God can act beyond these laws, he never violates these laws. This is because he is also a great economist.[87]

God is the perfect economist, never wasting energy or effort. He designed the universe to work as a system. We can observe the operation of this system and describe it using the laws of nature (e.g., gravity, speed of light, et cetera). God does not suspend these laws of nature in his operations. To do so would interfere with the running of the universe. There are other fundamental principles he may use we may not be aware of at all. When these are present and active, it may seem supernatural to us.

The ultimate principle is his power: he "spoke," and the world was formed. God will use the means of least consequence to accomplish his purposes first before using supernatural means. Does this mean God will use situations like locusts, drought, and fire, or does God cause them? The answer is both, as evidenced by examples of both in scripture. A word about power. Thermodynamics is the physical science that deals with the relationship between different forms of energy. The first law of thermodynamics is that energy cannot be created or destroyed but can be altered from one form to another. Economy is all about careful management of resources, including energy and power. God is the greatest economist of all time, all the while observing the laws of nature.[88]

Why are signs, wonders, and miracles important to life and ministry? First, because they are misunderstood. Second, because many people do not believe they are possible. Third, because if one does not embrace the reality of signs, wonders, and miracles, they will not be prepared to acknowledge or perhaps even recognize God breaking through when it happens. The chapters coming ahead will focus on why these thin spaces and whispers are important in our lives and to our ministry. What difference can they make? How should we respond to them? If we cannot hear God, sense his presence, or recognize when the Holy Spirit is boldly grabbing our attention, how will we hear him in the noise of daily life? We have pragmatically given examples; described how to determine, if possible, if they are genuine; and dealt with some common cognitive and spiritual objections. There is one more sphere of life that can hinder our understanding, which has to do with the intersection of our biology and psychology.

We are fearfully and wonderfully made.[89] King David uses

these words to describe us as an awesome creation of God, extraordinarily complex! Often, this complexity is illustrated as mind, body, and spirit or soul. In reality, these different descriptions are not segregated and interact with one another in beautiful ways. They are pulled apart here to illustrate the intricacies of our creation.

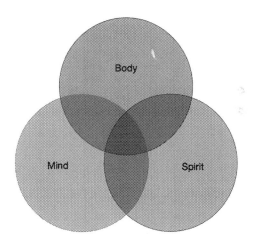

Our brain is the control center for all of this, to the point that a heathy brain (the organ) means a healthy mind. Here are a few brain facts that may surprise you and illustrate how our biology can affect how we think ... or fail to think. We are what we eat, drink, and breathe.[90]

+ The brain uses glucose from fruits, vegetables, and whole grains as its main source of energy. Too much junk food and sodas, and your thinking ability goes downhill fast.
+ The brain needs protein from eggs, fish, meat, milk, cheese, and yogurt to grow new brain cell connections. Most of the nutrients needed by your body every day are used by the brain. Poor connectivity between brain cells means the

structures of the brain have difficulty communicating with one another.

+ The brain needs omega-3 fats to produce melatonin, which insulates our brain cells and neural pathways. Too much of the wrong kind of foods, and we can short-circuit. It shows up in our attitudes and behavior. When you goof up, someone may say, "What were you thinking!" In reality, you probably were not thinking straight, and it is due to your nutrition.

+ The brain needs vitamins and minerals as well antioxidants to keep this marvelous organ strong.

+ Exercise produces an enzyme in our blood that travels to the brain. When we sleep, this enzyme triggers the production of a brain-derived neurotrophic factor (BDNF). BDNF stimulates the repair and replacement of brain cells and neuropathways. This and other chemicals produced through exercise improve cognition, learning, memory, self-control, and mental flexibility. However, this cleanup of trash in our brain only happens while we sleep.

Get the picture? Our physiology impacts our ability to reason or use logic, to keep things in perspective, or to exercise self-control. Nutrition, exercise, and sleep all impact our brain's ability to function well. Sometimes, our ability to apprehend and understand even simple things can be restricted by our health. Here is an example.

While counseling someone experiencing burnout, it became clear that lack of proper nutrition, exercise, and sleep was mimicking a serious mental wellness issue. They appeared to be deeply depressed and anxious, experiencing bipolar swings in mood and affect. What was really happening, it turns out, was physiological in nature, beginning with the junk food menu they had been consuming for years. As a result, they had developed a condition called hypoglycemia or low blood sugar. The brain needs glucose to function properly, and in its absence, it begins to function abnormally. This condition mimicked depression, and the momentary boost artificial sugars in junk food provided explained the mood swings upward and the corresponding sudden crash into despair. This went on long enough that this person began to question fundamental beliefs about who they were and who God was, since it seemed God hadn't been in touch for a long time.

When we are that worn out and tired, we can begin to question everything, becoming physically weary, and lose heart.[91] What began as a nutritional deficiency (body) began to drag on their emotions (mind) and cause them to question God (spirit). Since all three are integrated, this cycle could have started anywhere. Sometimes our inability to recognize God's presence in our lives is not spiritual, not our thinking, but physiological in origin. For this person, it eventually became a function of all three. The solution, however, was to straighten out their diet, get them back into a regular pattern of sleep, and engage them in regular exercise. The depression cleared up, and foggy thinking dissipated. They had renewed energy, clear memory, and a new self-awareness. Best of all, they realized God had not abandoned them, as they began again to experience the joy of his presence.

For nearly thirty years, we have served in risk zones around the world in the wake of natural disasters, epidemics, economic collapse, and other mass disasters, including war and violence. We work in the field alongside first responders, training them in caring for others and caring for themselves to avoid compassion fatigue and burnout. We teach in national medical universities, training health care professionals as well as developing curriculum, establishing course materials to train future medical professionals. We also provide public policy advisement in hope that the resources and education will be in place the next time a mass disaster occurs in these countries. We train pastors, teachers, and others how to set up community safety nets to provide relief in areas where there is little help or support available. Our teams have completed more than three hundred projects lasting up to two years in more than thirty countries, responding to earthquakes, tsunamis, hurricanes, epidemic disease, child and adult suicide, economic collapse, famine, poverty, civil war, and genocide.

We lead with service, allowing our host to take the credit. Our integrity and performance have won us invitations into places around the globe that generally do not want outsiders, especially Christians, inside their borders. We do not advertise and still receive invitations from ministries of health, education, and defense from around the world. Here at home, we work with veterans, health care professionals, and pastors teaching and coaching restoration to wholeness in life. This has expanded into church ministries serving pastors and staff worn down in the process of serving others and creating wholeness programs in their ministries.

What we encounter in this work is a deep longing people have for a certain amount of stability, certainty, simplicity, and clarity in life. However, life does not always cooperate and instead serves up volatility, uncertainty, complexity, and ambiguity. Sometimes this includes adversity, risk, and danger. This is largely our ministry environment on multiple continents. This ministry is prone to false starts, setbacks, betrayals; exposure to the elements, danger and injury, as well as illness; to say nothing of suspicion, misunderstanding, and discrimination. It has also saved lives, won victories, and advanced God's purposes beyond what any of us could ask or even think. What has preserved us and our teams through volatility, uncertainty, complexity, and ambiguity are the thin space breakthroughs and whispers when we were out of answers, worn out, lost, and didn't know what to do. Experiencing God's presence and listening to the Holy Spirit will preserve you through your life as well, leading you to the repentance, reconciliation, refreshing, renewal, recovery … whatever it is you need for wholeness in your life.

Our ministry of health, healing, and restoration to wholeness involves helping people learn to listen to the whispers[92] and recognize those thin spaces where God breaks through.[93] Because we capture more than fifty years of life and ministry with these stories, it may seem like God speaks to us in whispers and breakthroughs all the time. This is not the case. There have been many times in our lives when it seemed God was silent, some silent periods longer than others. However, we have experienced over time that his communication with us is persistent and unending.

God is always doing two things in our lives: dismantling something and at the same time restoring something. He has also given us the Holy Spirit[94] to guide us and help us understand what he has for us. If we are not listening, benefiting from these gifts can become difficult. Jesus Christ wants a relationship with us that fills up what is lacking, restoring our soul.[95] This idea of restoration pictures more than renovation and goes further to include restoring, or giving back, something to a former owner. Whispers, thin spaces, and miracles are part of this process.

7

FINDING RESTORATION

RESTORATION IS USED IN MANY ways in scripture—sometimes
as a noun, other times as a verb; sometimes referring to something
new, as in recently made, or renovated to a higher state of excellence,
or better in character or quality.[96] Restoration can occur in an
instant or can take a long time. In this chapter, we look at restoration
as a process that might include instantaneous elements alongside
longer periods of change, do-overs, and unopposed progress. What
is being restored is our relationship with our creator through Jesus
Christ. What was broken in the garden needs to be restored and,
where made possible by our free will, be completely finished when
we see our Savior in heaven for the first time—made whole, new,
and fully restored.

In the meantime, he is restoring our relationship with him
along the way. Jesus had a very public ministry, but his goal was
not to create a public image. He is about his Father's will. The

apostle Matthew takes care to point this out, referring to an Old Testament prophesy about the Messiah.[97] Isaiah, in describing Jesus's intent, says he will not break a bruised reed nor quench a candle wick ready to go out.[98] The crushed reed and smoking wick are devalued items of everyday use representing you and me. The reed and smoldering wick form a word picture for the spiritually, physically, and morally weak.[99] The victory for devalued people in this metaphor is the restoration of value.

Peter recognized his need for restoration rather dramatically the night Jesus was taken prisoner when he denied Christ three times, as Jesus said he would. It only went downhill from there for Peter, as things got worse and Jesus was crucified. From Peter's perspective, Jesus didn't come through when the chips were down. Even though he resurrected himself, he chose not to save himself in the first place. Peter was painfully aware of his own bankruptcy, and his view of the kingdom to come was all washed up.[100] There on the beach following his crucifixion and resurrection, Jesus restored Peter to ministry even though he knew Peter was scared to death of failure. Peter himself ultimately changed.[101] Peter was restored on the beach and yet had to grow into what that meant over time. Peter sums up this experience in helping the lame beggar at the gate of the Temple recover his ability to walk while also being refreshed by brand-new faith in Jesus Christ.[102] Earlier, as a disciple of Jesus, Peter was commissioned to be a "fisher of men." More recently, when Jesus appeared on the beach, Peter was instructed to build the church by caring for and equipping new believers. Peter has matured past the paralyzing fear of failure.

Restoration begins with the recognition of a fault, along with regret and repentance, accompanied by an earnest desire to be different. This reflects a change in thinking and turning to Christ in faith. This does not happen without the Holy Spirit's involvement. Yes, good people who are not followers of Jesus Christ in the truest sense can experience remorse and work at changing their ways ... but it will not produce salvation.[103] Restoration always requires some reconstruction, which is where the Holy Spirit gets involved. The good news is that restoration to wholeness in our relationship with God does not require perfection. Remember, it is a journey. A big part of this journey is the role forgiveness plays in our lives, forgiving ourselves and forgiving others.[104] We will get into this later in this chapter. Here is a peek at how we describe wholeness in our ministry.

THE HOPE OF WHOLENESS

Our goal is to bring healing, health, and restoration to people, families, and communities.

God's deepest heart is for our restoration to him in relationship releasing the full measure of the Holy Spirit's influence in and through our lives unhindered by our holding back nor ignored by our rushing forward.

Returning our lives to its owner, we are renewed in Christ, recognize our purpose, and learn to struggle well in managing our lives for the advancement of the kingdom and the Glory of God.

A healthy body, mind, and spirit including thinking, feeling, and acting in ways that create healthy physical, social, and spiritual well-being.

Restoration of our relationship with God can lead to restoration of other relationships as well. Our health physically and emotionally may need some restoration along with our spiritual restoration. There also may be a need to reconcile ourselves to certain situations, conditions, experiences, or failures. None of these possible needs are guaranteed resolution, and, in many cases, there may be a need from time to time to revisit some of these issues. This is why we describe restoration as a nonlinear process. It does not move in a straight line, always happen at the same speed, or produce results in our timing. The Holy Spirit, as our everyday guide, plays a huge part in this nonlinear process.[105]

There was a time in my life when I was terribly angry with several people who had let me down, manipulated me, and in some instances betrayed me out of impure motives. Pretty strong words, I know, but that is how I felt throughout a period of some months. In a whisper, the Holy Spirit reminded me to not defend myself, which became harder and harder over time. The Holy Spirit led others outside of this debacle without any knowledge of what was transpiring to encourage me. But it was a thin space experience the Holy Spirit used to clarify my thinking, find restoration in this breakdown in relationships, and let God have it his way.

I was driving to work one morning, chewing things over in my mind, becoming angrier by the minute. My thoughts were not kind toward these people. Out of nowhere, a voice spoke, saying, "I have shown you nothing but grace, kindness, and mercy throughout your life. You need to do the same for others." Wow! I stopped the car in the middle of the road. *That is so true*, I thought. Recognizing and regretting my faults in this power struggle (with them and with God), I repented on the spot and asked for help being a better person—one who would show others only grace, kindness, and mercy. It was a transformative moment in my life that continues today.

Ezra, in the Old Testament, is a great example of how nonlinear restoration can be. He was in the restoration business of people and nations. However, his part in the restoration of the Jews to their homeland began long before he was born. Israel had been conquered and most of their citizenry in and around Jerusalem deported to Assyria far to the north. The Babylonians had previously conquered the northern ten tribes in Israel and deported them north as well. Babylon followed and conquered the remaining two tribes in Israel of Judah and Benjamin.

The prophet Isaiah enters the story line before Cyrus existed and names Cyrus as the king who will release the Jews to return to their homeland.[106] When Ezra asks permission to begin the process of relocation, he references Jeremiah's prophesy regarding the specific timing of this return.[107] God had already prepared a way for restoration of a people and a nation to not only occur but take place at an aforementioned specific time. The Cyrus, the new king, as well as others in the community provided financing and materials for the trip and the rebuilding of the Temple. That is a lot to orchestrate over more than one hundred years. There were many times some would have given up on getting home or gotten excited and then disappointed when news spread there had been progress made, only to then be held up again.

Restoration is not the work of one person, family, or church. It includes many others as God orchestrates renewal. It takes a process over time to unravel and repair what may have taken a lifetime to fall into ruin in our lives. It is always God who moves the heart into a desire for restoration or even to just get help.

Those returning with Ezra knew their return would be opposed by those who took their place when they were deported.[108] Those who volunteered to return were fearful, vulnerable, doubtful, subject to shame and guilt. Recovery for individuals as well can be a journey involving embarrassment, shame, guilt, and vulnerability. God has an answer if we will trust him. Restoration will always be opposed by those who do not want to see a change in the status quo in someone, a family, a community, or even a nation.

There were lots of obstacles to overcome in the months and

years after the people returned. Competing agendas even among themselves, selfishness, the greed of those wanting to see Israel fail in their efforts to rebuild the Temple and the walls around the city, and the mistakes made along the way constantly created setbacks.[109] Nothing about restoration even under the best of circumstances moves forward without waiting, changing, and struggling. That is the nature of transformation. In our lives, as well as in the life of a nation, prayer is an absolute priority! During this time, Ezra is a great example of the importance of timing and his understanding that timing is in God's hands more often than it is in ours. Ezra somehow has a gift of balancing situational awareness with strategic perspective in moving forward, all the while understanding God will make a way using human instrumentality. So it is with our restoration as well.

King David penned one of the most famous psalms of all, Psalm 23. Verse 3 says of God, "He restores my soul" (Psalm 23:4 ESV). To understand what the goal of restoration is, one must consider what is inferred in this statement about being restored. To what are we being restored?

The word used here is one that refers to something we had in the past we need to turn around and get back to and pictures a process or journey back to a former condition. The object of this restoration is our soul, that part of our innermost being that is eternal. At some point in our creation, our soul had a wholeness that life can grind down, eroding confidence and self-image, producing moral injury leaving us wounded. Restoration constantly moves us back toward that former state, undamaged, not wounded, not weakened. This process is not over until we see Christ face-to-face. But wholeness in the core of our being can be experienced despite our circumstances. Wholeness is not perfection, which makes prayer, forgiveness of self, and forgiveness of others crucial to restoration.

It makes sense forgiveness should be a crucial part of our restoration because at the core of our being, restoration includes peace in our soul. When we are at peace with our situations, even the harmful ones, we have a level of peace. When I come to grips with the fact that all God has ever offered me is grace, kindness, and mercy, why wouldn't I then desire to offer that to others? Offering grace, kindness, and mercy is at the heart of forgiveness. When we understand we have all fallen short of the glory of God[110] and we are all in the same boat needing God's forgiveness, it brings our similarities more into focus than our differences.

Many therapists will tell you forgiveness is a gift you can give yourself. I can give a testimony on this topic, and I would assume many readers can share a testimony of this topic as well. Offering forgiveness to someone is a spiritual gift of maturity to you and me. It brings peace and contentment into our lives. When we are not holding on to a grudge, it is a huge weight off our shoulders. We benefit from this as well as the person we forgive. This does not mean they truly did not hurt you. Hurt is real. You and I may also need to put into place some strong boundaries around the relationship. How we interact with the person is completely different from what we do with the hurt.

Talk about freedom! Forgiveness brings so much freedom into our lives. Great freedom is found in forgiveness and is a critical part of our restoration with God. There are many steps on the journey to restoration. In fact, the steps may seem more like an emotional obstacle course on the road to restoration. The road to restoration requires strength, resilience, courage, and hope. It is like spiritual training on an emotional obstacle course. The more you run the course, the stronger you get. Yet along the way, you and I will be challenged by stress, pressures, starts, stops, blocked goals, unmet expectations, delays, and hurry-ups. All the back and forth may not seem like we are moving forward in restoration. Yet we are. Let us encourage you; even if you are facing an emotional obstacle course right now, you still can be moving forward even though it is hard, hurtful, and very difficult. Even if you don't feel it, you are developing perseverance, endurance, and strength. You are developing a stronger spirit and mind as you follow God's way through each obstacle.

What do you think when you hear James say, "Count it all joy, my brothers, when you meet trials of various kinds, for you know that the testing of your faith produces steadfastness. And let steadfastness have its full effect, that you may be perfect and complete, lacking in nothing" (James 3:2–4 ESV)? It may not be, *Oh good, woohoo, I am developing maturity!* Yet, in essence James is saying these hard trials are developing our spiritual maturity and lead to good things. This is one of the reasons people run from following God in hard situations. It is not easy, and it takes a committed believer to stick with it and change themselves versus asking God to change our circumstance. Sometimes God will change our circumstances, yet other times he has a higher plan for allowing us to grow and mature in ways we could not have imagined. God explains to us that if we want to be more like Jesus, we need to participate in the endurance and perseverance of this work ... his work.[111] Our goal is to struggle well as we partner with God in accomplishing what he is asking us to do to join in his purposes. This concept of "struggling well" can be likened to an emotional obstacle course. We keep going even when it gets hard. We may not handle everything perfectly; however, we still persevere and keep moving. When you pass over a high wall and move on to a mud run, it may slow you down. Nevertheless, you keep going.

The emotional obstacle course includes a variety of hurdles. One such hurdle is the ability to determine whether what we are feeling and experiencing is discernment or prophetic inspiration.

We talked about the importance of testing what we believe we heard from the Lord. This testing includes our ability to discern truth in a situation. This level of understanding takes us deeper into study and prayer. The ability to discern where God is leading is developed through practice. "For if you cry for discernment and lift your voice for understanding; and if you search for it as for hidden treasure you will discern the fear of the Lord and discover the knowledge of God."[112]

This is important, as this discernment and knowledge directs our paths in life and is not just knowledge to hold. Solomon, the author of Proverbs, understood the difference between seeking godly discernment and knowledge versus worldly discernment and knowledge. The knowledge and discernment of God is full of eternal purposes helping us in our daily decisions. When we partner with God and seek him, he will show us insight and help us see what is really happening in a situation. This is very helpful as we navigate the emotional obstacle course with God. When we have discernment and understanding, we can grasp what God is doing in our lives and not mistake that understanding as a prophetic inspiration or some sort of promise. It gives us courage and energy to keep going and to go in the right direction.[113] When I can see what God is developing in me, I gain more endurance and am not so confused with the why of a situation.

So why is discernment versus prophetic inspiration a critical element of growing in our walk with God? We may have a profound understanding in a situation, a longing or desire, and thus we discern what is happening, yet it is not something God has shared with us as prophecy regarding the future. We may understand and have an insight from God, yet he may not be telling us it is something that will come to fruition. Prophecy is a divine message from God. Prophecy from God is a truth that will come to fruition at some point in the future, a divine communication to a person or group of people. People are chosen by God to deliver a prophetic message. Peter explains a prophetic message is directly from God and is not of human wisdom.[114]

The difference between discernment and prophecy is vast and critical for us to understand what is really happening in our lives. God may give us discernment regarding our longing for something, yet God is not giving us any message about the outcome of this longing. When you are not sure if God is speaking to a specific longing, pray about it! Repeatedly pray about it and ask God to reveal if this is something we are discerning, or does God want to bring this to fruition? This is a complicated and emotional road because when we have a strong longing for something, we may overlap our desires with what God may be showing us is his will. Remember, we are seeking for it like a hidden treasure. This assumes there is some work to be done, and it might not be simple or quick.

Sometimes the difference between feelings and emotions can trip us up as well. We all share to some degree seven basic emotions. An emotion is a natural instinctive state of the mind arising from a number of different factors. They are part of being created in the image of God. As such, emotions have a volitional and experiential aspect. Anger is a basic emotion. It is both a choice and a feeling. Sometimes we cannot tell the difference since we move so quickly from choosing to be angry at one level while being overwhelmed by the feelings of anger at another level. We simply recognize it all as anger and often say to others, "You make me so angry!" Though they may have certainly done something to trigger your anger, in reality that is a choice you made. No one can make us angry unless we choose to be angry. Joy or happiness is another human emotion. It is also a choice we make that often results in a feeling we call happiness. We can choose happiness in the worst of circumstances. This is tough, really tough, sometimes!

But knowing we can separate a choice from a feeling can help us be more discerning.

The author of Hebrews informs us that in the last days, God will and is speaking through his Son and the Holy Spirit. The prophets of the Old Testament shared messages from God and delivered these messages to the people. Since Jesus's life, death, and resurrection, we now have the Spirit of the living Jesus Christ, known to us as the Holy Spirit, living in our hearts as believers. The Holy Spirit is now the one who both reveals and speaks the messages of God.[115] As we seek restoration in our life, we must seek discernment. As we mentioned earlier in this chapter, restoration always requires some reconstruction, which is where the Holy Spirit gets involved. When we deal with deep longings and grasp what God is doing, we have a spiritual ability to face our longings and allow God to heal and restore us. This is an important part of our purpose in life because what we may perceive is something broken in our life God is prepared to restore, returning it to its original state. All things will be restored in heaven to the place God intended them to be, yet God is committed to restoring us here on earth step by step, obstacle to obstacle, bringing us to a place of freedom and spiritual well-being. Restoring our soul, God is bringing healing, health, and restoration to people, families, and communities. This is the hope we cling to, pray for, and seek like a hidden treasure.

Obviously, this transformation means change. Change can be tough to accomplish, and some people choose not to change due to the difficulties involved. They may even choose the lesser pain of not changing over the perceived greater pain of changing. The truth is we must face the pain if we are going to be restored. A word of caution here: if someone you know is in need of transformation, you cannot force change on them short of an intervention that they still have to agree to. Ideally, you can come alongside others and win their agreement. Here are three principles regarding change when helping someone in a restoration process. People must choose to change for themselves. We can help create the environment conducive to change, but ultimately the choice is theirs to make. If you are involved in helping others through a restoration process, here are a few guidelines that will help you win cooperation, whether it is a person or small group you are working with in your ministry.

Lead with transparency. Recovery and restoration are a process over a lifetime. Be transparent about the gains to be experienced early in the process and the maintenance that may be required for a lifetime. We are all broken and recovering from something even during healthy occupational and social functioning. Encourage patience with the process of change. It is not an event and requires facing the pain.

+ *Set expectations.* People usually do not buy into something just because they are convinced. We find it easier to buy into something when we can predict the outcome. Change is not linear and can be iterative.
+ *Always be truthful.* If truth won't sell it, don't peddle it to anyone. Don't sugarcoat or minimize. Be willing to do and ask others to do hard things.
+ *Lead to a solution; do not lead with a solution.* Craft solutions together based on life information and relevant experience. Leave room for the Holy Spirit. Wholeness requires resisting evil and making the right choices. Teach that this is where true freedom is found and why the Holy Spirit within us is desperately needed.

Faith isn't the means by which we avoid trial. It is the means by which we stand up under it. Like the prophet Isaiah, we need to set our face like flint to sustain the weary with a word and not turn back.[116] Our faith is needed on the journey to restoration as we are seeking for it like a hidden treasure. Faith, commitment to the process, and perseverance are all needed as we look to God and follow his ways in finding restoration.

8

PRAYER

WE HAVE SPENT TIME LEARNING more about the deeply personal relationship God wants to have with each of us and some of the many ways he connects with us. We have also reviewed ways we can know it really is God breaking through and not last night's pizza or our imagination, expectations, or desires. Now we turn to discovering how these realities can make a practical difference in our everyday lives, beginning with prayer.

Prayer is the other side of a conversation with God, Jesus Christ, and the Holy Spirit. It is our side of the conversation and involves the Trinity. The Holy Spirit inhabits our prayers and expresses them for us even when we cannot find the words.[117]

Jesus Christ taught us how to pray and listens to our prayers.[118]

God hears our prayers and answers.[119] This may seem confusing and is not meant to carve out different roles for the

Trinity. The point is that when we pray, the Godhead hears our prayers and responds.

When Jesus taught his followers to pray, and through them we learn how to pray, he emphasized privacy.[120] There is prayer we participate in when we are with family, enjoying fellowship with other followers of Christ, and when we worship in church. These are situations where our prayers are often public. The conversation God wants to have with us, which Jesus is teaching his followers, is a private conversation. Two-way, not for anyone to hear other than the Godhead. A major part of this privacy is invisibility. Others cannot watch us, hear us, or be influenced by our practice. This is "God and me" time.

Invisibility is a keen part of the Christian's walk, and learning to pray in privacy is part of learning the discipline of humility as well. I have discovered in life one can have far more influence by quietly serving others, and less by trying to be a superstar. Like an iceberg floating in the ocean, the accomplishments and accolades others should see are there to see not because you put them there but because the rest of the iceberg, far greater below the waterline in your life, has pushed them up into the light. God will use the spiritual gifts given to us to serve others, even to accomplish notable things for others to see. For me, I am grateful for a career full of adventures, joy, satisfaction, toils that mature, and failures that produce resilience and resolve. The less the light is on me, the more it can shine on others. Our private prayer life is key to a humility that supports the rise of others while we leave our visibility and promotion up to God.[121]

Why would God be interested in a conversation in the first place? Jesus gives us part of the answer in a conversation he had with his disciples at a time they needed real encouragement, knowing he would be leaving them soon.[122] He calls them his friends, and through them, all who have come to know Christ personally through faith are friends as well. This word *friends*, as Jesus uses it, speaks to more than just a companion. This friend is loved. We are loved friends of the Savior! What is more, he has given us the Holy Spirit to help us understand the things of God that are ours forever through this friendship.[123]

In our private prayer life is where we often find God and the joy he has to offer us. Our prayer life invites God to reveal his truth and his desires for our life, yet it also engages us with him in a new, fresh way that produces joy. This invisible time with God can actually be our most fulfilling and joyous time of the day. Spending time reading God's Word and praying after we have read a portion of scripture brings new thoughts to life.

Paul in 1 Thessalonians mentions how the readers of this letter "became imitators of us and of the Lord, for you received the word in much affliction, with the joy of the Holy Spirit"[124] (1 Thessalonians 1:6 ESV). This scripture can be unpacked in many ways. One of the points Paul is making is by following the Word of God, interacting with God through prayer, and making our relationship with God a priority, we find the joy of the Holy Spirit. Connection to God through prayer literally brings joy to our hearts. We are meant to commune with God in prayer, and he blesses us in more ways than we can understand in his presence. Experiencing the joy of the Holy Spirit leads to contentment, patience, mercy, and understanding. When we experience the presence of God, we gain strength to offer others forgiveness, mercy, patience, love, and all the fruits of the Spirit. So we actually grow in our maturity as we pray, and our hearts are restored and refreshed as God heals us.

Prayer allows God to heal our pain and suffering. His joy covers and heals our wounds. When our hard situations draw us to pray, God can work in us and with us in powerful ways. For many years, I (Nancy) experienced headaches due to some hormone issues. Experiencing pain drove me to pray and seek God with a greater passion. The desire for healing was the greatest draw at first. I realized even in pain, lying awake at night allowed for a precious time of praying for everyone and everything on my mind regarding people who needed God's intervention. During this time, I also had a short list of focused prayers I would repeat and pray in the morning and when in pain. Over time, I saw God answering these prayers and strengthening me to handle current situations. My prayers included Jeff, our future, the kids, grandkids, family, church staff, ministry, international friends, and, if I was still awake in pain, it included reciting scripture in my mind.

Realizing my pain drew me to God in new ways inspired me to pray with greater passion and thoughtfulness as it drove me to God. My prayer life increased significantly, with a focus on the needs of others and my spiritual growth. In addition, God revealed to me how to walk with him in the middle of pain, not just seek healing. Allowing God to use this time and pain matured me in ways not expected. God as my strength, guide, helper, comforter, and advocate became more vivid. Mercy and empathy were other benefits I encountered. Pain had never really been a part of my daily life in the past; now I had a new sense of empathy for those who live with pain—and probably a whole lot more than I have experienced.

Listening to others with compassion allows me to serve them and come alongside them, relating and encouraging in ways I had not experienced in the past. Pain allowed God to bring good fruit from a hard situation. My new situation helped me see a bit more clearly how Paul could say, "I have learned to be content in all circumstances." Even when Paul was sitting in prison, he was okay because he saw a glimpse of God's bigger picture, knowing the Gospel was spreading rapidly while he sat in prison.[125] More people were hearing stories about the Gospel, stories of transformation and whispers of being put in prison for teaching the Gospel.[126] Paul says it became clear to him that what happened to him actually served to advance the Gospel, as the whole palace guard also heard about the work of Jesus. Sitting in prison, we know Paul penned a number of books in the New Testament, and the Gospel was advanced. What a profound lesson of God working in the middle of hard circumstances!

We can allow our challenges and pain to bring more delight to our lives when they prompt us to spend more time in prayer. Praying through our circumstances allows God to change, restore, and reveal more about himself and his ways. Prayer prepares us and enables us to handle what comes our way with more joy.

Seeking God in prayer out of a great need can lead to the unlocking of more spiritual truths and maturity than first intended. This is part of the mystery of God and the Holy Spirit. So much more can happen to our hearts and lives. Often, in prayer, I pray for a double portion of the Holy Spirit and an understanding of God's ways. As he enlightens me through the Holy Spirit, the Comforter, so many more spiritual insights can take place.

When I (Jeff) was new in my relationship with Christ, I still carried a great deal of skepticism about things like prayer. Why would he want to have a conversation with me? What would that look like? How do I know I am not fabricating what I think I hear in my imagination? Why doesn't he just speak up when he wants to talk to me? In previous chapters, we have seen how miracles, signs, wonders; impressions, insights, inspiration; people, events, and circumstances are all ways the Holy Spirit gets our attention. But let us get practical and look specifically at a conversation between us and Jesus Christ.

My mentor encouraged me to think about prayer as a conversation in which I expect a response without putting expectations on what kind of response. A typical conversation involves both speaking and listening. To be honest, my prayers were all about speaking, ending with an "Amen," and moving on. I wasn't listening for a response. So my mentor went further and encouraged me to respectfully challenge God to make himself known. There were two practical things to do.

First, I was to open my Bible, pick up my reading where I left off, and read a little bit to take my mind away from everything going on at the time. Try it for ten minutes was the instruction. Then begin to pray for ten minutes. Tell God what is on your mind. If there is something you are struggling with, be transparent about it. If there is something you don't understand, ask for wisdom. If there is someone or a situation you would like to pray for, let him know in detail. Find something to be grateful for and thank him. Ask him directly to reveal himself to you. Now take ten minutes to just sit and listen. You will be surprised what can happen next, or later in the day, or down the road that connects back to those listening moments.

Second, I was to start a prayer journal. So I took a small three-ring binder and filled it with paper. On each page, I drew a line down the middle. I recorded my specific prayer requests by noting the date and the prayer request in the left-hand column, leaving the right-hand column blank. As I continued to do this every morning as possible, I would review previous prayer requests. If I realized some had been answered, I put the date and the answer in the right-hand column. After a year of doing this, I realized there were incredibly consistent, specific answers to my prayers! I even ran some statistics (yes, my skepticism kicked in) to make sure this was not just by chance. Now I had evidence God was listening and responding.

During that period, the time I spent listening produced fruit as well—an impression or clear instruction emerging consciously; something in my Bible reading looking like it had a flashlight on it, encouraging me to dig deeper; occasionally a soft word or an encouraging touch; and more frequently a deep sense of his presence. This was the beginning of understanding what it means to abide in Christ.[127]

Jesus describes himself as a vine and us as branches in John 15. This description occurs in a context where Jesus is encouraging the disciples. He describes this connection as abiding in him and he abiding in us. This is a familiar phrase to the disciples since he previously described the Holy Spirit as abiding or dwelling in them, just as the Father abides in Jesus. The expression may seem awkward to our way of thinking today. The idea behind it, though, is not awkward at all. A vine provides nourishment to the branches, and the branches cannot bear fruit without being connected to the vine. We are the branches, and in Christ, we are connected to the vine. As long as we remain (abide) in Christ, we will bear fruit in our lives. John 15:7 attaches this idea of abiding in Christ to remaining in his Word. This is something that became a habit in my life, beginning with those first attempts to read, pray, and listen.

Prayer is a significant part of our sanctification and restoration journey. As we walk with Jesus day by day, he is continually interceding on our behalf.[128] When we don't know what to pray, we can ask the Holy Spirit to intercede on our behalf with the words needed regarding our concern. The Holy Spirit intercedes for us when we ask and even when we do not ask. The Holy Spirit prays for us in our weakness, lack of clarity, and when we don't know what to pray. Weakness here is related to our human limitations. When we can't see the whole picture or know exactly what is needed, the Holy Spirit knows what to pray. He searches our hearts and knows the will of God in every situation so can pray in accordance to God's will on our behalf. This all leads us to the well-known verse about how God works for good for those who love him and are called according to his purpose.[129] God will work out all situations for our good and for God's will.

As we seek God's will and purpose in a situation, we have bold access to approach him directly in all matters. We have both the freedom and confidence to approach the throne of God with our requests.[130] Jesus's completed work on the cross gives us bold access to bring all our concerns to him. Everything! We can bring every little and large need to his throne through prayer. We ask for strength, we kneel in humility, and we seek his will, all through prayer. What a gift! What a blessings beyond measure! What a thrill we can believe our prayers will be heard and answered. Then we can trust God will do immeasurably more than we ask or even imagine, according to his power at work in us.[131]

This blessing regarding the outcome of our circumstances is a promise from God. God's Word reveals he has promised to accomplish good according to his purposes. Purposes that are eternal and from the work of God.[132] Let me (Nancy) illustrate a time when God accomplished his purposes from one of my prayers. A number of years ago, I sensed we were going to move to a different area approximately thirty-five minutes away from our current home in Southern California. This potential move would put us closer to our home church, friends, and family. As I was praying about the situation, I sensed God said, "July." After finishing my quiet time, I ran downstairs to share what I sensed God was saying and told Jeff the details of my quiet time. Jeff immediately asked, "Which July?" This question stopped me in my tracks. What July? Well, I didn't ask. To make a very long story short, God did end up prompting our move two Julys later—two and a half years later. Yet he continued to do miraculous things for many Julys on into our future. We would notice something profound happening in our lives and realize it was happening in the month of July. What an adventure God has us on, showing us his promises and his miraculous hand on our lives!

As much as this time of waiting in prayer was both exciting

and challenging, sometimes God chooses to answer a prayer quickly, right in front of our eyes. One year, we were traveling to Africa to teach, serve, and meet with pastors, ministry leaders, and governmental officials. On our trip, there was a problem with a connecting flight from Brussels, Belgium, to Uganda, and we missed our flight to Uganda. The airline said they had rebooked us to go to Addis Ababa, Egypt. Jeff and I looked at each other and thought, *This will take us way off course and get us there too late for the first conference.* We stopped and prayed for favor to get on a flight to Uganda for a quick refuel, then on to Rwanda our final destination. We asked if there was any way to spend the night in Brussels and take the first flight out in the morning. At first, they said no; then a different ticket agent overhearing the conversation said, "Well, wait. The Joneses just gave us back their free night at a hotel here in Brussels and took another flight, so we have a free night stay at a hotel close by, and you can fly out in the morning." We said we would take it. Prayer answered! We ended up having a beautiful dinner in Brussels and a good night's sleep at a lovely hotel, and we flew out in the morning. This answer to prayer was a blessing in many ways because it actually helped us arrive fresh and ready for the conference to start. God knew this delay was actually a gift and an immediate answer to prayer.

Sometimes these "arrow" prayers in the moment end up with an immediate answer. An arrow prayer may be a quick, short prayer in the middle of a busy day. They may occur amid a crisis or traumatic situation. In the middle of a conference call recently, we were discussing the direction of a new ministry and felt a little stuck. We stopped and asked the Lord for guidance, direction, and his will in this situation. Then we went back to work discussing a variety of options. This pause actually calmed us all, put the focus back on God, and allowed our thoughts to seek his will versus just getting the project completed. There are many examples of an arrow prayer, including praying for safety for our kids, spouse, or family, relief from pain, wisdom, and the list could go on.

Long or short, our prayers are conversations with God. They refocus our attention on surrendering to his will, bring a calmness, and allow us to look to God for guidance. When we remain in God like John the apostle talks about, our faith in God grows as our trust increases, and we see God work in our prayer life in powerful ways.[133] This prayer conversation with God can be passionate when we are in the middle of suffering or as simple as a needed flight connection at an important place and time.

God chose to place his Son as an infant into a human family. He did not leave him on the side of the road to be picked up and cared for as an orphan. He didn't place him into a wealthy or noble family who would be able to provide great care. He placed Jesus in an ordinary family so that someday Jesus could place us in his heavenly family. This also resulted in Jesus experiencing life just like we do with all its ups and downs, trials and tribulations, joys and sorrows.[134] How else could Jesus relate to us if he did not live in our world, experiencing all the same things we experience? So when we pray, we can make it personal just as we would in a conversation with our best friend.

9

FILTERS AND BIAS

GOD WANTS A RELATIONSHIP WITH us to the point he reaches
out to us in ways that respect our social paradigm, our culture,
and all those things in our lives that make us who we are. He
wants to be understood. What makes it so difficult to understand
him then? For me (Jeff), it is not enough to say Moses and Elijah
wanted to see and understand God, but God didn't show up in a
humanly visible form because to look upon God evidently would
have resulted in their harm if not death! We know from scripture
that God met with Moses at the gate of the Tabernacle regularly,
and Elijah heard God in a whisper. God showed up outside
Abraham's tent with two angels looking like three men and sat
down to a meal together. Why is a conversation so hard for us to
imagine and enter into?

It could be attributed to doubt or unbelief, I suppose, or simply
not paying attention. We have seen examples of the lengths God

will go to get our attention. For those who long to connect with Christ in a deeply personal way but do not have that experience, there are two factors to consider that form and shape how we receive those attempts to get our attention. Our personal filters and biases get in the way.

We naturally run what we see and hear through our mental filters. Examples of common filters are beliefs and expectations, emotions, circumstances, differences in social paradigms and culture, and our own unconscious, self-protective behaviors. Our understanding is shaped by what these filters strip out of our context. Our reality consists of the things we strip out of our thinking as well as those things that remain. To see reality more truly, we must recognize we have filters and work at understanding their impact on our understanding of people, places, and things. The apostle Paul left Titus on Crete to complete the process of church planting they began together. It was a tough job, especially since Cretans had a reputation for being lazy, evil gluttons.[135] Yet as we read further, the truth of the matter was that the cities in Crete also had good people in abundance, who Paul challenged Titus to enlist as elders in the new churches. For some, the reputation of the Cretans acted as a filter, shaping their opinion of the country as a whole.

Filters also shape our faith. A number of us were visiting an Eastern European country and had been invited to a meeting in the Ministry of Defense to discuss an event senior military leaders wanted to produce with our help. It was controversial for them, and there was wrangling going on regarding pros and cons of even considering such a thing. Bruce and I were selected out of our group to meet with a few of the general staff and participate in the discussion. We arranged to meet our group outside the building after the meeting.

The building reminded me of our Pentagon. Tight security

inside and out, thick bulletproof glass on the entrance kiosk windows, armed guards everywhere, stationed at doors and elevators and roaming the building. We were given photo identification cards on lanyards and admitted. We were escorted to an elevator that took us to our floor and were delivered to the conference room. The meeting did not last long. No agreement among anybody seemed to be possible. We were escorted back, turned in our passes, and left the building.

We joined our waiting group and gave them the news that there was going to be no conference. Amid the expressed disappointment and questions, Bruce said we should pray. So we gathered a little closer and prayed quietly, trying to not look like we were praying. When we were done praying, Bruce remarked, "God spoke to me while we were praying!"

Yeah, right! was my condescending thought.

Someone asked, "What did he say?"

Bruce, who was our leader, responded, "He said to send Jeff back in there and get us a conference!"

To which I responded in disbelief, "So you, in effect, are saying the Holy Spirit told you to use the old line, 'Here am I, Lord, send Jeff'?"

When I reached the security kiosk, I realized I had turned in my identification pass. Standing there waiting for the guard on the other side of the glass to end their conversation with someone inside the booth, I saw my lanyard sitting on the countertop. At that time, the entrance door opened, and a number of uniformed individuals exited. Meaning to pick up my pass from the inside, I walked in just as the door was closing. The guard just inside the door did not stop me. The guard in the kiosk was still in conversation, so I turned around and walked toward the elevator, wondering what the two guards there would do.

Just as I approached, the elevator doors opened, disgorging

a large group. As they passed, I slipped in. No one said a thing: no shouts, no stampede in my direction, no shots ringing out … nothing but the soft sound of the elevator doors closing. On the trip to my floor, there were no alarm bells ringing that I could hear, and I wondered what the two guards would do when I got off on my floor. Actually, they did nothing, and I assumed they recognized me from just getting on the elevator previously and probably didn't notice as I passed by so quickly the absence of my photo identification card. They did not notice either that there was no armed escort.

When I arrived at the conference room doors, there were no guards at all. Knocking on the door and sticking my head in, I was greeted with a room full of surprised faces. One of the generals said, "Good, you are still here. If you had left the building, you would never have been allowed back in." I also learned that without an escort, I should have been arrested immediately. If they noticed my missing identification, they said nothing. I was invited to sit down and continue the conversation.

We reached an agreement. The conference was a huge success. Over the next decade, doors were opened across the continent for ministry that is ongoing and still growing now forty years later.

Here is my problem. Very familiar with stories of miracles in the Bible, this event brought to mind the story of Peter escaping prison because an angel showed up, his shackles fell off, doors opened before him, and the angel escorted him past guards and out of the prison.[136] At that time, I had real difficulty taking this story at face value. I did not believe it happened this way and perhaps did not happen at all. Yet here I was in the middle of a similar experience, where I should not have been able to come and go with freedom. There was no angel involved, or restraints, or doors moving on their own. But what did happen was a drawing of attention elsewhere that allowed all those guards to miss me passing by coming in and going out. My filters kept me from believing this was a thin space where God broke through according to his purposes in my life. In addition to my filters of unbelief and distrust, there were my biases that got in the way as well. In fact, many of our filters are a reflection of a bias.

Biases can be cultural, sociological, or demographic. They can be based on stereotypes, memories, our family upbringing, our education, and especially our selfishness. A bias can be a prejudice against a place, a culture, a people, or a way of life. Bias distorts perception and does not allow for differences. The language in this country mystified me, and I didn't trust interpreters. Lots of bias there to throw up walls of self-protection. The Holy Spirit would eventually work this out of my system as well as the unbelief that gave it power in my life.

The challenge of not dealing with filters and bias is that we also filter out God's efforts at communication with us. Our biases prejudice our understanding, and our conclusions become distortions of truth. Even worse, they affect our intuition and empathy by limiting our ability to see patterns in our own life or to identify with others in a way that enables us to come alongside rather than avoid or confront. We become egocentrically locked into our way of thinking, being, and doing, as if it is the only right way. We lose all neurodiversity.[137] Yes, this is a real word and is used to describe the way people experience and interact with the world around them in many different ways.[138] There is no right way of thinking, learning, and behaving when it comes to being a healthy person. Fortunately, our everyday guide, the Holy Spirit, helps us understand and respond constructively to our filters and biases. This help shows up in different ways, including convincing us of truth,[139] convicting us of how far off from the truth we may be,[140] and encouraging our change of mind.[141]

The apostle John gives us such a wonderful picture of just

how intimate and personal a relationship with God in Christ can be.[142] In his letter to the church at Laodicea, John uses a beautiful metaphor picturing Jesus joining a family meal and entering into a long-held custom of fellowship with closest friends. But first he knocks on the door asking permission to enter the home. Jesus forces nothing on us in his efforts to have a relationship with us. We always have the choice to let him in or not. Avoiding that choice can get in the way of being able to see or hear the knocking. If we take the initiative to seek him out, to invite him in, Jesus will respond. In fact, he encourages us to seek him out.[143]

This concept of being pursued is not new to the New Testament. We find this idea in the Old Testament as well.[144] If we seek him, he will be found. The invitation does not have to be like Moses's burning bush, or Abraham's visit from strangers, or Elijah's whisper in the storm, or Jacob's dream of a ladder from earth to heaven. It more often comes through the Holy Spirit enabling us to recognize when God breaks through in the most ordinary ways.

Sometimes in our seeking God, it is our intellectual understanding of God that gets in the way of belief and faith. If we want to draw near to God, we must believe he will respond. This is not only important for our relationship but key to knowing God's will for us. Some people adopt a shopper's attitude and take the position of wanting to hear what he has to say before we decide if we are going to buy in or not. Willingness to do God's will is a prerequisite to even knowing what that will is in the first place.[145]

The solution to this is to simply ask the Holy Spirit to make God known to you no matter what he has to say. Let him know you want a personal, vibrant relationship despite your doubts, reluctance, and desire to control the outcome. Persist in this request and then practice listening.

We can engage more specifically in this process by actively

working to adjust our filters and remove our bias. The apostle Paul uses the expression of put-off and put-on to describe what we would call replacement therapy today.[146] Putting off an attitude, habit, way of thinking or acting requires some degree of de-habituation. Habituation has to do with a decrease in response due to repetition. I used to live about one quarter mile from a railroad crossing. Late at night, the train would come through sounding its whistle, and the guard arms at the crossing would come down with their clanging bells. It was a terrible noise, to say nothing of the train rumbling through close enough to feel the vibrations as it passed. It didn't take too long before none of that woke me up, and I was sleeping through the night. I had been habituated, desensitized. Examples of desensitization include unconscious habits that need to change, promptings of the Holy Spirit that are repeatedly ignored, poor responses to people or circumstances that continue unnoticed by us but not them, unconscious bias impacting our thoughts and behaviors, and triggers we do not recognize that cause unhealthy reactions in us.

Putting on, or replacement, is simply a matter of substitution. We need to identify what needs to change (the Holy Spirit helps with this) because it is unfruitful to mental, emotional, and spiritual growth and substitute good thoughts and behaviors for unhealthy or destructive thoughts and behaviors. Prayer, time reading and studying the Bible, scripture memory, journaling, and fellowship with believers all help in this process. You may need to use breathing exercises to calm yourself, giving yourself time to recognize what you were thinking, what you were about to say or do that should change. Replace what needs to change with what should fill the desensitized space in your life it has taken up. Give it time, be persistent, and break the chains.

Our ability to recognize a personal filter or bias can be based on our past experiences, temperament, or just how we are wired.

We have been intentionally created by God, and this includes our design, purpose, and spiritual gifts. Our design, purpose, and gifts will also affect our responses to each situation. God has specific plans for each of us. How we view life through our filters and biases actually affects our daily thoughts and actions. God understands our bias and filters and is continually working and speaking to us in order to accomplish his plans in our lives. Understanding God has specific purpose for each of us throughout our lives helps us to keep seeking God. This ongoing desire to always be in God's will inspires us to continue the conversation with God.

As we are reminded of this aspect of our life, we will see how God is drawing us to himself. God is saying to us, "Here I am," standing at the door of our heart, wanting to hear our invitation to enter. He is continually saying, "Here I am."[147] Just like in the Bible, we have friends and neighbors who knock on our door, and their desire is for us to be home and to answer the door and invite them in. This example of hospitality is an illustration of how we need to have an open heart to God's purposes.

God initiates an ongoing relationship with us, yet we have a role to seek him out in response. As we seek to understand our spiritual gifts and how best to use them for eternal purposes, we get to know God better. We ask God, "How should I use this gift?" This desire of ours to use our gifts requires a conversation with God in prayer, listening and action. Jesus's life is the greatest example of living a life according to the purposes of God. John 3:16 is a beautiful picture of how the life of Jesus is one of sacrifice and love. Jesus gave his life for us according to God's will so we can be reconciled to God. Jesus is an example of no greater love, no greater invitation, and no greater sacrifice when it comes to his relationship with us.

God's desire is that the world be filled with his glory, reconciling all thing to himself and bringing wholeness into our lives.[148] When we love like Jesus, our actions fill the earth with God's glory. When we follow God's ways, it fills the earth with God's glory. This is in part visible and part of the mystery of the Gospel. Our obedience is both seen and in ways unseen.[149] God is continually reconciling us to him and all people to him.[150] This is an aspect of restoration. God, in drawing us to himself, is restoring a relationship with him that was meant to be all along, even from the beginning in the Garden of Eden. He has a plan of restoring us to the relationship with him that was designed from the very beginning. This restoration involves restoring our life to wholeness, to joy, and the ultimate healing through salvation when we get to heaven. Healing is what happens in the moment of salvation and continues throughout our life on earth.

One of the most important places we restore our walk with God is in our marriage and family. As we grow in spiritual maturity and grow in our ability to love, we apply this to our marriage. We grasp the importance of serving our spouse and sacrificing for God's purposes. In a marriage, we each have equal value yet different roles. God has a purpose for our marriage and a purpose for each one individually. We are placed in the church with gifts to use for eternal purposes, not selfish purposes. Our marriage is one way we exemplify the body of Christ in how we love, serve, care, and encourage each other.

One of the most destructive applications of bias and filters is comparison—if we compare ourselves to others in the sense of how we are doing: are we doing better than they are doing? Our bias toward ourselves has a built-in, self-protective filter, which will always give a false sense of progress. If we compare ourselves with others, it can lead to self-boasting (pride). Often it can lead to a strong desire to want more power, more prestige, more possessions so we can be like others we envy. The best comparison to make is to Jesus and how we are living up to his call in our lives. The promise of scripture is that if we put Christ first in our lives, those things we truly need will be added to our lives.[151]

When it comes to bias and filters, which we all have in some form, the Holy Spirit is our guide. Our thoughts, intuition, and empathy are all subject to our bias and filters. The Holy Spirit can give us understanding, convincing us when we are right and convicting us when we are less than right. We need to be listening, open to change. Our design, purpose, and even our spiritual gifts equip us for life lived out in the presence of others. God has a future and a hope for every single one of us he wants to unfold in the context of a relationship with us. We need to be listening, open to adventure. Christ places us in the body of Christ, the church, where we fit best and will find peace and contentment. We need to be listening, open to discovery.

10

DOING LIFE TOGETHER

WHEN WE EXPERIENCE GOD PLACING us in the body of Christ for us to grow, mature, develop, and serve within the context of God's purposes, we gain clarity about why we are at a church serving the people God has intended us to serve. We see God's call on our life to help and serve others as well as personally strengthen us in our walk with God. Paul, in Philippians 1:6, says that God will begin a work in the life of a believer and has a plan to finish this specific work. God continues to develop us and help us complete this work through the gift of the Holy Spirit, who dwells in all believers. The Holy Spirit is our guide, helper, counselor, comforter, and our Paraclete called alongside us. He comes alongside us with whatever we need in our lives and offers comfort, guidance, help, direction, instruction, and peace and teaches us all things. His presence is a comfort, both in our heart and mind. He encourages and calms our emotions and our thoughts. In a world full of much adversity, pain, and trauma, we need a savior who gives us vision by supplying all our needs.

This encouragement can often come through those who we love and are doing life together with us. While writing this chapter, I (Nancy) went through a minor skin surgery requiring a bit more work than expected. It took us all by surprise, yet God had my heart and comforted me in many ways through our small group. We prayed together, texted prayers to one another, and lived life with all its changes and hassles together. God comforted and encouraged me through these people and answered prayers through them as well. Any worries that tried to creep into my thoughts were interrupted by prayers, songs of praise, and acts of love from our small group.

God's mercy came straight from him as well as through the dear friends he put in my life as a gift directly from his hands. God's favor and mercy includes doing life together with a small group of people. Whether it is a health issue or direction in life, we petition God together, we agree in prayer, and we even struggle a bit for the answer together. Our role is to personally seek God alone, be in his Word, and counsel with close family, yet adding to all these elements a small group of God's people coming together is both thrilling and a blessing from him. God loves us through others and shows us such care in tangible ways. I can't imagine not having this spiritual support system in my life now.

In fact, we have been designed for these kinds of relationships. I (Jeff) love to teach neurobiology to students learning more about mental wellness and the connections between our biology and psychology. For one reason, it demonstrates how sophisticated and often beyond explanation we are as human beings. This is especially true when it comes to our brain. The complexity of the layered connections and functions of the different structures of the brain demonstrates elegant design and the statistical improbability we evolve.[152] For another reason, it provides an explanation for why we are better together.

Without interaction with other people, brain cells (neurons) die off. Each of us needs others who will seek us out, show interest in us, and help us experience safety, security, and significance. We have a social brain that needs others, all of us looking for those connections that provide meaningful relationships with others. The interpersonal biology involved in connecting with others in ways that shape our brain is fascinating. Not only because it protects against apoptosis (the death of cells, which occurs as a normal part of our brain's development) but because it provides an explanation of how we change and why this happens best through learning and through relationships. Here are some mind-bending insights.

When we exercise consistently and with some intensity, an enzyme produced in our muscles flows through the bloodstream to our brain, where it triggers the creation of a brain-derived neurotrophic factor (BDNF), which, in turn, stimulates the replacement and repair of brain cells and neural pathways respectively. But this only happens while we are in deep sleep. Think of our brain as if it were an office building. At the end of the day, all of the people who work there go home. A short while later, during the night, the janitorial staff shows up and cleans up the offices for the next day, just like the work done in our brain. This helps us understand why exercise and sleep are important to brain health. The energy for this work comes from the food we eat. Bad diet, bad brain, so to speak. Nutrition, exercise, and sleep are as important to mental wellness as are meaningful relationships and purposeful work.

Now I am sounding like my mother! Eat right, exercise, get the right amount of sleep, keep good company, and find purpose in your work.

Learning involves changing the brain. More literally, it requires the building and repair of neural pathways. For the brain to produce new brain cells, it needs more than good nutrition, exercise, and sleep. It also needs stimulation. Mild stress provides stimulation, while moderate to high stress and trauma can lock up the brain due to the effects of introducing epinephrine into the bloodstream (adrenaline). That is when hypervigilance, elevated heart rate, and a sense of foreboding distract us from learning. The process of converting perceptions into longer-term memories, a key part of learning, comes to an end. Active learning requires involvement in activities that stimulate multiple connections in the brain. Experience, especially relational experience, is also a key part of learning through stimulating the development of new neural pathways, which is key to changing our thinking.

Interactions with others change the internal biochemistry of brain cells, which triggers creation of new neural pathways. It is way more complicated than a single sentence can convey. The result demonstrates how the brain changes in response to experience. In fact, our brain is constantly changing in response to what we experience throughout life. This demonstrates incredible design and purpose. Human beings have also been given a soul to inhabit God's crowning creation, and God wants to have a relationship with us that is eternal. The body, not so much, but the soul is eternal, and God's earnest desire is to have a relationship with us right now. The body of Christ (all followers of Christ) are part of the Church with a big C. The church with a small "c" is how we refer to those fellowships of Christians doing life together where that experience can continue to encourage one another, growing together.[153]

A few years ago, we were in a small group, and one of the women in our group was pondering a move. Aside from the desire for her to remain in the small group, we authentically and genuinely sought God's direction for her life. She asked us to seek God with her. She wanted to hear what those who knew her well thought. She respected the wisdom of the group and the years of walking with God some brought to the group. A few in the group were new believers as well, and they offered their thoughts and watched as this played out. So together we prayed as we discussed and sought God's best. We all had a sense now was not the time to move. The job wasn't quite stable enough, and her living situation had its flaws.

It was one of the most beautiful moments when everyone was in one accord and helped her think it through. She put the move off due to these and many other factors. It wasn't until years later the Lord put all the details in place and made it clear the move was in his plans. What a beautiful experience to see God work though an intimate set of friends committed to God's best. It requires wisdom, discernment, and godly knowledge of those offering advice, yet when a small group seeks God together with a genuine heart, God does and will move and plays an important part in both encouraging us as well as offering guidance.

We go through many shifts in life, and having a group genuinely seeking God together is like a guardrail helping us navigate life's trials, challenges, and decisions. A small group may be one of the most important influences in our life for staying between the guardrails walking the narrow road. Not everyone will make decisions based on God's best, so having a group that will encourage us in supernatural ways is how God can speak to us directly. God often confirms his direction through others.

Another example of God working and speaking through a small group happened to us a number of years ago. We were part of a small group that had been together for many years. Some of the couples had watched the kids of group members grow up from toddlers to departing for college. One day, the men in our small group had plans to get together on a Saturday morning for breakfast. As the men showed up at one of the couple's home to give the husband a ride, the wife greeted them at the door totally panicked. Her husband had just collapsed and had not regained consciousness and passed away moments later. It was one of saddest moments the group had experienced together. The loss of this precious friend was devastating to the wife, two boys, family, our small group, and the many friends this man had made over the years. It shocked us all. One of the sons was in college. This small group of friends knew God was asking us to step up and help. We could give you more details, yet we believe this thank-you letter years later tells the story better than we could. Here was the letter we received from one of the boys. Everyone in the small group received this letter.

> Dear Jeff & Nancy: I'm writing this to you from a place that I never thought I would be. Losing my father was the most difficult experience I have ever gone through, and nothing could have prepared me for such an event. This event was taxing not only on my family's emotions (obviously), but also on our finances. Suddenly it seemed like there could be a chance we wouldn't be able to make it through the next year. Thankfully, I believe in a God that will always provide for us no matter how horrible life may seem. We prayed daily and God opened up more hearts than any of us could have ever expected. I am where I am today because of your contribution. There would be no celebration for my graduation if it wasn't for you. Words cannot describe how truly blessed and thankful I am. Thank you so much from the bottom of my heart;

this degree belongs not only to me, but to you as well. Sincerely, Alex [not his real name]

This letter still stirs deep emotion. This small group was exceptional and blessed, extending to not only those who attended the small group but to each family member and child. This letter is exceptional, written out of a love for God, deep emotion, gratitude, and maturity. His ability to understand how God supplies our needs through others is uncommon. This young man knew the value of community and experienced it firsthand. Life changing! We all experienced God working through this life event.

The apostle John, writing late in his life to the churches he was responsible for, gives his readers some sound advice born out of much experience.[154] He cautions them against becoming too attached to worldly things. The world will come to an end someday, but our relationship with the Father is eternal. This creates a paradox! How can we successfully live in the world but not be worldly? This is where doing life together alongside other followers of Jesus Christ helps us discern those fuzzy boundaries between worldliness and godliness. In other words, right living in a broken world takes prayer, wisdom, and understanding the heart of God. The Holy Spirit is involved as our everyday guide. But there is one obstacle that many struggle with while not understanding why they struggle regarding our hearts and minds.

If God wins someone's heart, he will win their mind as well. But if God only gets someone's mind, it is unlikely he will win their heart. This is because many who come to understand and intellectually assent to there being a God fail to go further and enter into a relationship with him. For lack of a better term, we could consider them cultural Christians. They participate in all the cultural norms for being Christian and respect the social mores, celebrations, and practices associated with their respective faith tradition, but they have no idea what it means to have a personal relationship with Jesus Christ.

Having been raised in the church, that was my (Jeff) experience until the day came when I surrendered my heart to Christ, not just my mind. Up until then, I knew about God but did not know God. Now, we cannot be judgmental about this matter and consider those who do not reflect our same values or understanding as having only an intellectual understanding of belief in and obedience to (in other words authentic faith) our Savior and therefore not having a personal relationship with God. That is never in our provenance to determine. This question of a relationship is personal, for you to decide for yourself and not for anyone else. This is where the Holy Spirit comes into the picture, leading us to and helping us understand who Jesus Christ is, what he has done, and the response he desires from us. If we draw near to God, he will draw near to us.[155]

Many have begun a personal relationship with Christ early in their life but have found themselves much later living with less zeal, less passion, and less sense of connection. This definitely is not a matter of cultural Christianity but more a symptom of drifting away from the relationship you once experienced and still exists, only at a distance. This is where renewal comes into the picture, and renewal usually starts within a group.[156] This is why the concept of iron sharpening iron is so critical when it comes to understanding the difference between worldliness and godliness. We often have similar struggles on the side of worldliness.

In our small group recently, we talked about how not to be too attached to the things in our homes and releasing these desires to God. When a group of believers discuss this concept in humility and together say we are all trying not to find our identity in our home or possessions, we make great strides in not allowing these pressures to influence key decisions in following God. For instance, in choosing to go on a service trip to Africa instead of purchasing possessions, we loosen our grip on the things of this world. When a small group of believers is discussing these types of challenges, we are influenced in profound ways to live according to God's purposes and let go more of what ties us to worldly things. Shifting from worldliness to godliness takes a conscious decision in the heart of individuals willing to be humble. The ability to make these types of decisions most often comes from a heart of humility and a contentment with our current situation. God revives us from the inside out and brings us back from where we have drifted away. He will lead us, heal us, and restore our relationship with him. We will know peace, not as the world knows peace but the peace of God that helps make us whole and restored.[157]

Sometimes in the face of suffering, loss, and grief, we question why God has allowed something to happen. We may feel abandoned, wondering if healing will ever come physically, emotionally, or spiritually. These thoughts and emotions are a part of being human and tempt us to blame God for our pain and loss. Often, we walk away from God in these dark times. When I am tempted to give up, I tell God exactly how I feel, from the heart, not just the mind.[158] I seek grace to see God for who he really is in the middle of this circumstance, asking for strength to take the next step and to teach me how to seek refuge in him. We live in a broken world among sinful people. One day, all things will be reconciled to Christ, set right as you will. Until then, we all will have troubles in this world.[159] But Jesus Christ has overcome the world. The beauty of a small group in these times is they can help us run toward Christ, not draw away from him. Difficulties that test our faith to the extreme are thin spaces God can break through, comforting us with his presence.

When we feel abandoned by God, wondering if healing will ever come, how do we understand what is truly happening from

God's perspective? We know God wants good to come from all situations, and we know from the scripture God is in control of all things, even though he does not cause the evil in the world that may rock our circumstances. So one of the first steps we can take is to go to the scriptures to understand these concepts. What do we truly know about God and his character? We can also go to God in prayer to seek wisdom, insight, and guidance. In the middle of a hard situation, we seek God and develop an even stronger relationship with him, versus pulling away out of frustration. Yet how does this practically work itself out? As an example, let me share the story of when I was experiencing headaches due to some hormone changes. It was a few years into experiencing both migraines and daily hormone headaches, and the pain was not going away, even with all the prayers for healing by family, friends, and our church.

One day, the realization came that there needed to be a shift in my thinking. Even if the pain did not change, the main issue was how to walk with God every day in the middle of the pain. Prayers shifted, asking God to teach me what he would have me learn as I walked with him in the pain. It was a huge shift in my thinking, and it gave a whole new experience of joy and peace in my walk with God. My thinking is what changed the most and confidence in God grew as I looked at the situation differently—placing hope in the unseen because of assurance of God's character. When I shared this experience with our small group, others in the small group were profoundly affected because a few in our group had been facing chronic pain. We together kept asking ourselves, *How can I walk with God in my current situation even if nothing changes?* Our prayer life increased exponentially. When in pain, we found ourselves praying for everyone on our prayer list, including all the other issues in our life. We never expected pain to draw us to such a beautiful place of extended times of prayer. It was like our pain was a reminder to pray, seek God, and draw near to him. A shift from frustration to prayer was ignited. This adverse situation drew us to one another and to a deeper, more intimate relationship with God, which seemed almost miraculous.

11

CONTENTMENT

CONTENTMENT IS BOTH AN EMOTION and a choice. It is both biological and psychological. It is a neurological response to stimuli in the limbic region of our brain, which we experience as one of our most fundamental emotions and at the same time a volitional choice we make to be content, or not, in spite of circumstances. This is more than a little confusing for me, since I grew up learning from experience that happiness and satisfaction, and therefore contentment, were a result, not a choice. Boy, was I wrong! It is actually the other way around; contentment psychologically is also a choice and not a result. Here is why this is true.

Emotions, in the sense of mental health, are tied not just to our psychology but to our biology as well. It is a two-way street with body impacting mind and mind impacting body. This is why experts tell us a healthy brain means healthy body and mind. At the same time, we can make decisions that enable us to regulate our emotions. Take anger for example. It is one of the strongest fundamental emotions we can experience. Yet anger is also a feeling we can choose to manage. There is a well-developed professional specialty, *anger management*, built around this concept of exercising volitional choice in order to manage our anger. In fact, we can manage all of our emotions in a manner that does not allow them to manage us.

I (Jeff) am usually pretty even keeled and content in spite of circumstances, but not always. Here are my contentment confessions: I am a disabled veteran and not always happy or satisfied with that condition. By education, training, and temperament, I can be a perfectionist at times, which can get in the way of my acceptance of circumstances and people. By profession, I am a healer and need reminding occasionally I cannot help everyone who comes to me for help. You see, like most people, it is ultimately my limitations that become the focus of my discontent. Living with and accepting our limitations is key to contentment. Contentment is a state, not a trait, and experiencing contentment is a process, not an event. Commitment to the process of repeatedly making good decisions can keep us in a state of contentment longer and diminish the impact of uncertainty in our lives. As often as you can, choose to be content. Your feelings will eventually follow that lead.

Contentment may seem to be an odd subject seemingly unrelated to God breaking through and getting our attention in life. Actually, it is discontent that is the disrupter. Sometimes we can get in our own way due to our feelings of discontent. Discontent can not only rob us of contentment, but it can render us deaf and dumb to what God may be trying to say to us. The apostle Paul describes contentment (the state of being content or at peace with one's circumstances) as something of great gain.[160] The context for this remark is the discontent some experience as feelings of envy or greed. These emotions can lead to bad choices.

However, not all emotions or feelings are bad. In fact, emotions are a part of being made in the image of God. Part of God's design includes the ability of emotions to inform our reasoning, just as reasoning should inform our emotions. This is why, neurologically, when we make an informed choice, both are involved to the point that our emotions will eventually line up with our reasoning.[161] But when we make decisions based solely on our emotions, our reasoning will not line up in support, and we find ourselves constantly justifying ourselves to ourselves! This is where the Holy Spirit can step in, reminding us it is the Lord who weighs (measures) the heart in an ethical as well as emotional sense.[162]

If contentment is both an emotion and a choice, what about inner peace? Since contentment and other emotions are both biological (our brain is a physical organ) and psychological (our thoughts and our feelings), we can apply the same concept to peace. Peace has both biological and psychological elements. It is a two-way street with body impacting mind and mind impacting body. When we enter a distressing situation, we have the choice to remain calm and peaceful. Our mind can instruct our body to remain calm in the middle of a distressing or uncomfortable situation. Spiritual disciplines, including prayer, can prepare us to handle adverse situations with a calm spirit and mind. The reality that there is a spiritual dimension to life (we have a soul) plays into this dynamic interaction of brain chemistry, thoughts and emotions, and the presence of God.[163]

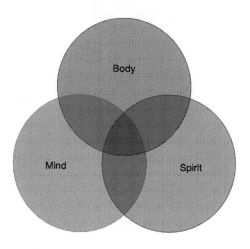

A definition of solace I (Nancy) find intriguing is peace in distress and God's comfort and inner peace in our loneliness. Both contentment and solace can be a state of mind we choose amid challenging situations. As we lean on God and allow his gifts of comfort and peace through the Holy Spirit to flood our thoughts and emotions, we develop strength and discipline to handle adverse situations calmly. This allows us to make informed and wise decisions with a calm attitude. Our emotions are still engaged and active, yet they are informed by our thought process. God's solace or peace will allow us to remain calm.[164] This ability to remain calm directly affects our ability to be content. When we know God is working in all situations to bring about good, we can remain both peaceful and content.[165] They are intertwined. A peaceful feeling is directly tied to our contentment.

When we are experiencing both peace and contentment, we can still be unhappy about a situation. When a devastating situation arises in our life and we rely on God's presence to calm us in distress, we don't have to be happy with the situation. We can still be content and have faith God is in control and will bring good out of the situation. When was the last time you saw someone handle a hard situation well? You probably said to them, "You are dealing with this so well," and maybe they responded that God is blessings them with a peace that surpasses understanding.[166] We can wish a situation was not present in our life yet be content God will use it and will show us how to navigate through the situation, even if we don't understand what he is doing. This is also a thin space where God breaks through with new understanding, new insight.

I was not happy during the skin surgery creating a scar on my face, yet God drew me to himself as scripture reinforced how God is concerned with the status of my heart and my intimate walk with him. If a health issue is going to draw me closer to him, and God does not take it away, then I can choose to walk through the situation with a peaceful heart and mind.

Many times when a circumstance makes us unhappy, it seems like a distraction to us, when in actuality God is using it to teach us an important lesson on our spiritual journey. We can be unhappy about a child accepting a job or even a call to ministry in another country that limits our time together. Yet we can find in this trial contentment and peace, knowing God has greater plans for their life. God has plans for our children that are full of a hope and a future, and sometimes this makes us very uncomfortable and maybe very unhappy.[167] Dealing with difficult circumstances and even conflict in our lives is one of the many ways God develops our spiritual muscles.

My (Jeff) first job right out of college was as a plant engineer for a very large chemical manufacturing company. Responsibility included directing the work of electricians and instrument technicians in keeping the plant running night and day. Actually, there were two foreman who really did that work as they trained me. One day, a critical machine broke down, and the decision was made to manufacture the piece needed for repair in order to get the plant up and running as soon as possible. The project was given to me, and I really wanted to make a good impression.

Checking constantly on progress, I found one of the foremen in the back of our shop heating a pair of shears to red hot and then plunging them into a tub of cold water. I actually thought they were taking time away from what needed to be done to work on a home project. You can imagine my response and the sharp remarks I made. They kept on working while I kept on speaking my mind. Running out of things to say, he turned to me and said, "The part we need to make as part of the repairs is made of stainless steel and very hard. We have nothing to cut it with, so I am tempering these shears so that they will be stronger than the material we have to work with."

Without another word, he went back to heating and dunking. Uh-oh. I felt a thin space coming on! Sure enough, it seemed almost as though the Holy Spirit was pressing his weight down on that remark, impressing me that this is exactly what God is doing to me in this job and in this moment—preparing me to be ready to handle difficult situations in a future career in health care I had no idea was going to be part of my journey. Our ability to stay calm, full of peace and contentment, is an important part of God's way of strengthening us to deal with the purposes he has for our life. It is a sign we are maturing and growing in our walk with God.

Feelings follow volition is a difficult concept to get across to some people. Part of the reason for this is the role intuition plays in our decision-making. Intuition is the ability to understand something quickly without the conscious benefit of reasoning or logic, though those attributes may have been working subconsciously. Good intuition is part of emotional intelligence and the ability to sense or know the right thing to say or do in a situation. Our sensitivity to social cues, body language, tone of voice, and even our past experience can play into our intuition. The result often is an on-target observation or sense of things, which is difficult to defend to someone else when asked how we arrived at our observation. It seems to them, and perhaps to us as well, that we are being led by feelings.

Here is what is actually happening: our brain is a social organ that develops through interaction with others. Our experiences, especially with others, create changes in the chemistry of our brain at the cellular level, which activates a process of change in our developing brains.[168] We adapt and build new neural pathways in response to experience. Another way of saying this is that our thinking changes in response to our experiences, both positive and negative.

The Holy Spirit is a part of this process as well, convincing us and convicting us as part of helping us navigate life. Most of the time, it is in a manner so indistinguishable from our own thoughts we can miss this thin space if we are not looking for it. This relational process also changes our thinking and our emotions. Jesus promises peace, not as the world understands peace but a peace characterized by total well-being, a sense of security, and contentment.[169]

Throughout our lives, a variety of situations will arise challenging our way of thinking. Sometimes a situation calls for a calm attitude, yet other times situations arise stretching our understanding and stimulating a new way of thinking about a subject matter. We sometimes call this "stretching" cognitive dissonance when we are thinking through a new way to solve a problem, adopt a new concept, or seek an alternative outcome. Let me explain with a very simplistic example.

Remember the days when you would only eat peanut butter and jelly sandwiches on white bread? Maybe you were a young child when this occurred. Then someone offered you a peanut butter and jelly sandwich on wheat bread. What was your thinking? *How can this be? The best PB&J is only served on white bread!* The dissonance between what you experienced as the right way to serve up a PB&J sandwich and what you are now being offered meets with doubt, resistance, and perhaps even rejection. You may have felt pressured to try PB&J on wheat bread in order to not create conflict. Your mind was in a process of cognitive dissonance. Eventually, you adjusted your thinking about wheat bread and actually enjoyed this new way to serve up a PB&J sandwich.

We do this all the time in life. Whether it is white, wheat, gluten, or gluten-free bread or more high-stakes decisions like whose job is it to take out the trash in your family. You have some inconsistent thoughts, beliefs, or attitudes as they relate to behaviors or decision-making, and you alter your position due to overwhelming evidence, resulting in changing your mind. You see, our minds like congruence, balance, peace, and the absence of conflict. Our brain is biologically wired to minimize confusion, discordant thoughts, and ideas that challenge current thinking and the status quo. Yet, as we are exposed to these new thoughts again and again, over time we move in the direction of either eliminating them altogether or shifting our thinking to accept the new idea. The dissonance goes away.

God works in our lives in this way often when he is growing and shaping us for new purposes or a new direction. He has given us free will to accept a new shift in our lives or to reject it. To follow his ways or put off following his ways. Our ability to accept a new circumstance in our life and be content with the situation is critical to experiencing contentment. We can choose to accept adverse situations with peace. This new sense of acceptance comes as part of a process involving putting off the old and putting on the new.[170] Seeing God break through our stubborn or old way of thinking and reveal a new, better, more profitable way of serving him is no simple breakthrough. This is often why the Holy Spirit plants a seed in the form of a new idea that contradicts or challenges in some way something we are holding on to that needs to change.

This is a profound moment in our lives as God patiently waits for us to adjust our thinking and shift from old patterns to new ways. This is evidence of how God creates a thin space in our lives as it relates to our thoughts and behavior patterns. Like comparing the Holy Spirit to the wind, we feel it, sense it, yet don't see it fully, yet we know it is there and God is working even when we don't see it with our eyes.[171] We feel the weight of a circumstance yet can't quite put a finger on what is being asked of us. As we wrestle with new spiritual concepts in our walk with God, he is breaking through—guiding, shaping, and drawing us to a new place in our walk with him. He is patient and kind and knows our ways better than we know our ways. How have you seen God do this in your life recently? This type of thin space may actually create a huge shift in your life. The first sign this may be happening is the dissonance of clashing ideas or an unsettledness or lack of harmony with something you previously felt strongly about but now question.

God can use discontent, dissatisfaction, and dissonance in our lives to interrupt our sense of inner peace and contentment in order for us to struggle well with getting back to that place of solace in our thinking and feeling, as a prelude to new things in our lives. Human problems can and do crowd out the sense of God's presence with us, even when he is standing next to us.

Late in Jesus's ministry, the disciples finally understood who he was, the Son of God. Peter made his great confession, and they had witnessed great miracles, including seeing Jesus come to their rescue walking on the water, and this after feeding the five thousand! Now Jesus had one more lesson for them, and for us, in raising Lazarus from the dead.[172] Jesus and the disciples had retreated to a place of safety because of those who sought his death. A quiet, out of the way place where they could lie low for a while. Word comes that Lazarus is sick. Jesus waits two days before leaving for Judea to see Lazarus, who by then has already died.

The disciples were surprised that Jesus was willing to return to the very region people were hunting for him! They were reasonably worried those same people would kill them as well. Thomas, who was the group's skeptic, even said sarcastically that they should all go with Jesus and die together. Human problems crowded out of their minds the reality that Jesus Christ, the Son of God, was literally present among them. They were content and at ease where they were staying one moment, and in the next, they were discontent, very dissatisfied with this plan, and at odds with the idea that they should leave this place of safety for one of avoidable danger. Quite the dissonant options out of sync and harmony with each other!

At the beginning of this chapter, we described contentment as an emotion and a choice. We also described discontent as a disrupter that God often uses to get our attention. How do you handle this kind of disruption when it comes? Certainly we may feel resentment or even anger at the intrusion into an otherwise safe, comfortable situation. That is a normal emotional experience. But do we make a choice to be content in spite of circumstances? Do we listen for what the Holy Spirit has for us in those moments? Do we really believe God is present with us? These disrupters can often be the whispers that get our attention and swing our focus around to what he has for us in this situation.

God's timing is always linked to his purposes. We may recognize in our discontent something of his purposes and what we can do to be content. However, recognition of an opportunity is not the same as a necessity to act immediately. There may be a bit of struggle to get back to where contentment is restored. We need to choose to struggle well if that is the case. By making that choice, we will see our feelings fall in line behind our will and keep us moving in the right direction with peace that passes all understanding.[173]

Someone once said that we don't *have* a soul. You *are* a soul and have a body.[174] God wants a relationship with us and is committed to our journey toward wholeness in that relationship, no matter where we are in life. He wants to speak to and with our soul, our innermost being, in building that relationship.

12

WHEN GOD IS SILENT

ON OUR JOURNEY TO WHOLENESS, the road will entail twists, turns, highs, lows, triumphs, failures, adversity, and setbacks. God speaks and communicates to us in a variety of ways through all these circumstances. In our walk with him, he is always making a way for us to grow. When he is making a way for us in the wilderness, he may choose a form of silence to draw us to him. He has a plan! God may not communicate in a way we are used to hearing from him. He has a future mapped out for us, yet for a time, this may include a different and purposeful form of communication. Silence, in the sense of communication, has a purpose and does not mean God has turned his back on us. When Jesus promised the Holy Spirit to the disciples, he made sure to assure them of his love and that he would continue to reveal himself to them.[175] That is his promise to us as well as believers.

God truly is never completely silent. He still is speaking through creation, such as sunsets, mountains, flowers, blue sky, oceans, and rocks. Where we find beauty, we can find God. God's heart is to always connect with us in ways we can experience his presence.[176] On the road that goes down to the Mount of Olives, the Pharisees were asking Jesus to silence his disciples, and in response, Jesus said that if the disciples would not praise him, even the rocks would cry out.[177] The main concept Jesus is communicating is even if people will not confess or praise Jesus for his works, creation will praise him, acknowledging his authority and power.[178] We should never assume that the ordinary holds no message for us.[179]

God speaks through scripture. So even if we sense the Lord is silent, we can find his words in scripture. The prophet Isaiah gives us a picture of God doing something new in our lives. When God is doing something new, he often uses a new way of communicating. When God makes a way in the wilderness, he asks us to be on alert for his presence in a new way, to not be fearful, to realize he is with us even as we walk through adversity. He says to acknowledge him as our God, to realize we are precious and honored in his sight. He loves us. Grasping the importance of this statement gives us courage, confidence, and purpose.

A number of years ago, we sensed God was getting us ready for a new season in life. We were changing churches, many people in our life were moving away, and life felt a bit unsettled. This continued for a while. It became a bit frustrating. We made sure we were reading a lot of scripture and allowing God to speak in our quiet times. We were continually encouraged by concepts in scripture on movement and new seasons in life, yet no specific details. We realized God was strengthening our ability to be flexible and mobile. He was expanding our capacity to live in the unknown and to go where he said to go without a lot of notice. It was a new rhythm for us. It kept us on our toes and actually drew us closer to God in order to follow his ways. God was actually moving us forward in our walk with him.

So when God is making a shift in your life and rhythm, pay attention. Recall the times God has spoken in the past and see how they may apply in the moment. Remember his grace from the past and let it evoke gratitude now. Put some extra effort into prayer and being aware of what God is doing. Through, prayer, scripture, and his creation, seek God even in the frustrating times, when it appears God is silent. We are his children, and he says he will never forsake us.[180] He may actually be moving you forward in your walk with him. However, the waiting for an understanding of why the silence can at times be frustrating.

"When? Just tell me when!" Though we do not often say those words out loud, most of us think them loudly while waiting on God to speak a word of timing or direction, or delivering a blessing we have been praying for, or providing relief from a very difficult circumstance. But all we get is silence. We (Nancy and Jeff) have had these experiences consistently over the years. Sometimes it has been waiting for the word to *go* related to the timing of entering a new job or ministry, or moving to a new place, or the right moment to bring a message of importance to someone. Sometimes it has been related to the suffering of loved ones emotionally and physically, and we are looking for solutions, relief for them, or even just a reason why this is happening. Sometimes it involves struggles with our own health as we are waiting for healing. But the silence is deafening, and we wonder why God is silent.

Waiting when you know the timeline is not as hard as waiting without knowing anything about timing. Nancy and I knew our turnaround work in the church we were providing leadership for was coming to an end. We needed to be looking for a new senior pastor to take the church into the future. Sitting in a midweek pastors' community meeting one morning, I felt a tap on my shoulder. Looking to the left, I didn't see anyone trying to get my attention. Perhaps I just imagined it. Just at that time, a pastor to my right spoke up, and at the sound of his voice, I knew he would be my replacement—just a feeling but very convincing.

When the meeting broke up, I went over to where he was sitting and introduced myself. We agreed to meet for coffee. Eventually, we became good friends, and I continued to keep my thoughts regarding his possible future to myself, waiting for God to open the door to having a conversation with him about our need for a new senior pastor. Time dragged by with no unction from the Lord to say anything. Was I mistaken? There were some good things happening in his own church that needed attention. Would inviting him to consider a new role ruin a good thing in progress? More than a year went by, still waiting. Then the state claimed eminent domain over the property they were using for church, creating the need to find a new place to meet.

The waiting was over. The freedom was there now to broach the subject of having their church join ours on our property. Both congregations agreed. We worked out a transition plan and installed the new pastor with everyone's approval. The church continues to do well under their new leadership. God was putting together a plan far more elegant than anything we could have invented. The silence on the issue of new leadership was broken.

There are lots of reasons beside just working things out that make it appear to us that God has withdrawn his attention. Silence has a way of providing an opportunity to evaluate our journey with Christ and possibly to bring on a new sense of humility as we look inward for reasons. We slow down and take stock while being slow to speak and quick to listen. For me (Jeff), silence can mean that God recognizes an unwillingness to obey. He will show his will to those who are willing to obey his will.[181] There are times when silence is due to something completely opposite from our resistance. God is pleased with us and knows we can trust him through the silence. There is a passage of scripture that pictures these tensions beautifully.

Israel is threatened by her enemies and trying to find some nation they can forge an alliance with that can protect them. God, through the prophet Isaiah, warns them to repent of this idea and trust him for deliverance.[182] After all, he has delivered them many times before. In his appeal to Israel, an interesting word is used to describe the solution. This word is *quietness* and is not often used in this manner. It communicates a sense of absolute silence in being still, undisturbed, with total confidence in God while they wait. The test for them and for us is whether we are willing to wait. Our strength will be found in the silent trust we offer in confidence that God has our best interests at heart and will hold us up.[183]

Our ability to live out a silent trust with God is an important part of our faith journey. When I (Nancy) think back on the times it felt like God was silent, the realization comes he was actually working in the waiting. God was preparing my heart, strengthening my endurance, allowing me to struggle well in this new shift, and bringing me along in my ability to trust his ways and plans. God was setting up details for his perfect plan. Just because I was uncomfortable did not mean God was not working. In the waiting, what felt like a form of silence from God was actually a season moving me forward in my walk with him. A time of waiting or wilderness is often associated with stretching times. God is still moving in our life; yet all the details are not evident or obvious. It takes faith and trust to keep seeking God and his ways. We need to surrender any demanding thoughts hoping to ease the uncomfortable. The desire to get out of this season is strong. It takes an attitude of continual surrender, love for God, and a strong stance of knowing he has the best for us. Even when we want to challenge him, he knows what to do. We all have experienced an attitude of not being sure God really knows what he is doing. He does. God's thoughts are so much higher than our thoughts, so much grander and more vast. We really want God's ways; they just are not easy to endure at times.

You may recall my story (Nancy) of God waking me up at midnight one evening, and I sensed he said, "Go." God was asking me to leave Southern California and move to Colorado Springs, Colorado, with the company I was working for at the time. They were moving their headquarters to Colorado Springs, and I was being asked to make the move and lead my team in publishing throughout the move. California was my new home. It did not feel great to uproot all the good found in Southern California, including a great church, a strong spiritual community, friends, family, and weather allowing a lot of outdoor exercise, play, and enjoyment. God was asking me to go. The move was difficult and awkward and included many disappointments. Settling into a new life, routine, and work had its challenges. Years into the move, I was still waiting for God to move in new ways and show me why he had me make this move. Those years were rough and uncomfortable. Then … I met Jeff. Cindy, my sister, had said, "I think you are going to meet your husband there." She was right. After years of waiting, wondering what God was doing, I met my husband. He is the best gift on the face of this earth I have ever experienced from God's hand. A miracle. In the waiting, God was growing my trust in him; my quiet times became deeper and required me to cling to God in new ways for guidance and direction. Since my community was much smaller, my dependence on God was greater. God did have great plans. He was actually moving me forward in my walk, trust, and faith in him. It was a powerful lesson of following his voice and letting him work out the details and orchestrate how the miracle will unfold—a profound lesson in my life to this day.

Sometimes silence is a time for working out something new

in our thinking. God gives us space to do this kind of rethinking. My (Jeff) father grew up on a farm. As a youngster, our family would visit relatives who were also farmers. One day while out in the vineyard, Dad noticed some outbuildings some distance away that were painted green, matching the color of the vines, which made them hard to pick out in the first place. He asked what those buildings were. The answer he got was "They are barns." My dad simply said, "No, barns are red." What followed was a long conversation about the right color for barns. It rose to the level of an argument.

In my dad's day, and the days of my grandparents and great grandparents, there were no paints that stood up to the weather as well as paints mixed with iron oxide. However, this mixture always produced a tinted version of whatever colored paint was used. So manufacturers simply added red to the mixture, and thus all barbs as far as the eye could see were red for most of Dad's lifetime. The norm for Dad was red barns. But science had moved on, and other more environmentally appropriate colors could be used. This idea significantly challenged his cultural norm when it came to what color a proper barn should be.

The red paint served a useful function in his day and became the form everyone used. At some point, this form no longer was the only way to serve the function of protecting the barn from harsh weather. Form follows function. Often when one form or another no longer serves the function for which it was created or is no longer the only way to serve that function, people will still hang on to the old forms for longer than necessary. It is part of their cultural norms. It took Dad a while to come to grips with this reality, but he eventually embraced the change and was fine with green barns.

Sometimes there are situations in our lives that need a new way of thinking—a new approach, new attitude, or new application.

This is true for all of us. It can become challenging to filter through our biases, old habits, and cultural norms when confronted with a need for biblical change without being conformed to the world. However, it is God's nature to insist on change, while at the same time it is our nature to resist change.[184] Resistance can be a good thing when it comes to things that should not change.

Jesus gives us a very practical example of the three dimensions of needed change.[185] Some things should be dropped, some things should be changed, and some things should remain the same.

Jesus heals the blind man by making clay out of saliva and spit. Saliva was viewed as a remedy of sorts in those days but not mixed with dirt. In fact, no had ever heard of anyone healing someone blind from birth. Jesus is accused of healing someone on the Sabbath and allowing that person to work on the Sabbath (making clay and picking up his pallet and walking off was considered prohibited work). This prohibition is not found in the Old Testament but came from the rules and traditions of the Pharisees, which Jesus consistently challenged as inappropriate and not needed.[186] Finally, Jesus tells the healed man to go to the pool of Siloam for ritual cleansing. This was also a time where the healed man could be examined by the priests and cleared to rejoin the community. Jesus rejects form (healing on the Sabbath), changes form (using saliva mixed with dirt), and validates form (ritual cleansing providing opportunity to rejoin the community).

Sometimes silence is a time to work through something needing to change in your life. We find all that is needed for this kind of self-reflection in scripture.[187] The journey toward wholeness in life is not a journey toward perfection in this life. It is a journey requiring change along the way at different times and in different ways, while Jesus remains the same yesterday, today, and tomorrow.[188]

The Trinity—God the Father, Jesus Christ the Son, and the

Holy Spirit—clearly demonstrates commitment to making it possible to have a relationship with us. These terms have been used differently throughout this book where roles commonly ascribed to each are in focus. This commitment is also demonstrated in the many ways that enable us to experience God breaking through into our lives. Nature, life circumstances, signs and wonders, other people, church, fellowship with other believers, sanctified intuition, prayer, personal encounters, suffering, crisis, sanctified memory, practical faith, life transitions, and even silence are just a few examples. In illustrating these with our experience and the experiences of others, we have also exampled why many people do not recognize when God is present in the moment or the season. All of this against the backdrop of scripture, which speaks to these situations and conditions.

Jeremiah is a great illustration of multiple ongoing encounters with God that were transformational in his life.[189] He often uses an expression that is common in the Old Testament when introducing something God communicated.[190] The general idea behind this literary form is there is a self-existing influence that shows up at times who can change things in our lives. We know from the New Testament that this influence is the Holy Spirit.[191] Thin spaces have the power to change our lives. Just as we have had to answer the question for ourselves, what are you going to do when God shows up in your life?

The book of Jeremiah chronicles his forty-year career as a prophet to the tribes of Judah and Benjamin. The northern ten tribes have long since been taken into captivity by the first worldwide power, Assyria. Babylon is soon to replace Assyria as the global power, and Jeremiah lives under both regimes and their brutality. His world is in turmoil, and the only solution is to seek God in repentance for their decades-long rejection of anything having to do with God. Instead, Judah seeks a treaty with Egypt to protect them against the invading Babylonians. Unfortunately for Judah, Babylon defeats Egypt and lays siege to Jerusalem, just as Jeremiah said they would.

A world in turmoil, with everyone looking for solutions but not from our savior, Jesus Christ, who through the Holy Spirit is constantly reaching out today in the same way God did in Jeremiah's time. Jeremiah's story comes to a close, but our story is continuing with God still seeking a relationship with us in Jesus Christ our Lord, through the direct efforts of the Holy Spirit. In Christ, we have purpose and meaning for eternity, which we have and are being equipped for right now.[192] So, what are you going to commit to when God shows up in your life? Ask and he will answer in the clear, even when it may be silent. You will know. After all, it is the Holy Spirit's role to convince you.

Thin Spaces has been about recognizing when God breaks through into our lives, getting our attention, drawing us closer, and revealing his heart for us. This connection can be transformational.

Jeremiah the prophet was sent by God to the potters' workshop, where he learned a lesson about transformation from watching the potter work the clay (ESV).[193] There are times when the potter isn't pleased with what is taking shape in the clay, but he does not give up on the clay. He reshapes the clay into the very image of its purpose. God was illustrating for Jeremiah, in the middle of all the things that were not changing in his circumstances, God was still for him and that he can change his will based on our behavior. Transformation only comes through relationship with Christ. Do you need a little reshaping, a little restoration to wholeness? Allow the Holy Spirit to guide you back to that thin space, where you can choose to engage with the one who loves you still.

13

RESOURCES

WE HAVE INCLUDED A FEW resources we used in developing material for this book. The illustrations may be helpful to your understanding of some concepts touched on but not discussed in depth.

THE ROAD TO WHOLENESS

Experiencing wholeness in our relationship with Christ is a journey, a process, and not an event. Some people describe this journey as sanctification or maturing in Christ. We like to describe it as discipleship. In our ministry, we come alongside people where they are in this journey, providing encouragement and help for what comes next. Restoration occurs on the road to wellness in the sanctification process.

MENTAL WELLNESS

A healthy response to what life brings our way requires an ability to adapt well, having a positive perspective, mindset, and motivation. Motivation is energy we direct toward perceived needs. Sometimes we can be investing our time in things that will not be helpful to adjusting to circumstances, restoring perspective, having a positive attitude, or restoring our energy. One or more of the bubbles illustrated may need more attention than it is getting in order to get back on track.

HIDDEN SHOALS FOR DISCONTENT

Shoals are underwater obstacles like sandbars or reefs that can suddenly upset us and rob us of contentment. Sometimes it is clear to us what the cause of our discontent is. Other times, it may not be so obvious. It may be something related to a past trauma that triggers a mood change. Or it could be something related to your present physiology: nutrition, exercise, and sleep habits. Issues with your state of mental wellness, including meaningful relationship and purpose in your work, could be involved as well. After you give it some thought, you may want to jot a note down on the illustration page. Keep doing this until a pattern emerges that you can respond to with action.

STRESS DISORDER PATTERNS

Stress fatigue and other conditions related to stress can emerge as patterns. Often, we do not realize how a pattern of adapting poorly to life events can develop without our awareness, but it can and does. This can lead to a change in perspective, producing a negative mindset. You may begin to notice a loss of motivation or energy. This illustration provides more information about these patterns and provides some symptoms to help you identify where you may need to take action.

A PRAYER OF SURRENDER

When we find ourselves further into the process of stress fatigue, brain fog can set in. We want to get back to a place of clear thinking and renewed commitment to what is important in life. At times like this, a prayer of surrender may be a place to start. Unsure of what to do, simply use this prayer to guide your conversation with God. Yield everything and everyone to God as you pray.

THIN SPACES PRAYERS

Keep this nearby to selectively pray each day as you begin your day spending time in God's Word. Take ten minutes to read your Bible, ten minutes to pray, and ten minutes to listen.

THE ROAD TO WHOLENESS

Forget about what's happened; don't keep going over old history. Be alert, be present.
I'm about to do something brand-new. It's bursting out! Don't you see it? There it is! I'm
making a road through the desert, rivers in the badlands.
Isaiah 43.18-19, The Message (MSG)

Introduce them to Jesus Christ
Get them started in discipleship
Help them discover design, purpose, and calling
Teach them how to struggle well in managing their lives
Do these wherever you find them on the road

MENTAL WELLNESS

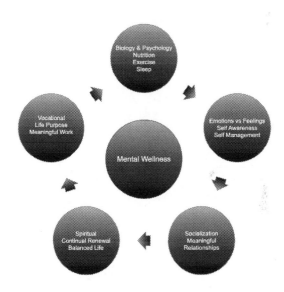

Hidden Shoals for Discontent
We tend to look at contentment and discontentment as circumstantial and passing without understanding these are not only a response to external influences, but even more responsive to internal influences.

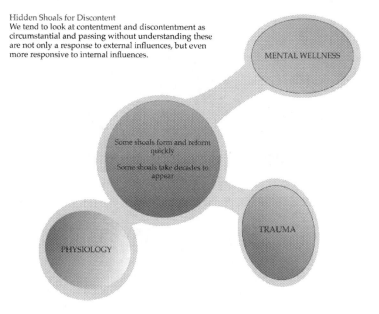

MENTAL WELLNESS

Some shoals form and reform quickly

Some shoals take decades to appear

PHYSIOLOGY

TRAUMA

Stress Disorder Patterns

Adaptation
Life and work events are a mix of stretching and nourishing experiences. Cumulative stress is associated with both. Poor adaptation produces stress fatigue and the beginning of burnout.

Perspective
There are nine clinical indicators of positive and negative mindsets. A predominately negative mindset degrades motivation. Impulse control and self-regulation of emotions diminishes.

Motivation
There is little energy to direct toward self-care. The neurology of burnout has a visible effect on the frontal lobe and limbic system producing cognitive impairment, depression, anxiety, self-medication, personality disorders, and suicidal ideation.

Crisis
Complete physiological and psychological collapse.

Most people adapt to change with little difficulty. However, constant change combined with other factors can erode resilience and lead to signs or indicators of emerging problems related to:

> Immature Responses
>
> Outbursts of Anger
>
> Discouragement and Depression
>
> Anxiety and Panic Attacks
>
> Addictive Behaviors
>
> Physical Illness

Most often this appears as unusual or unexpected behaviors you usually do not observe or experience when around this person.

Stress fatigue and stress disorders can begin to appear once someone's mindset shifts generally from optimism to pessimism. Characteristics that may signal this shift include:

> Out of Touch with Reality
>
> Increasing Conflicts
>
> Poor Decision Making
>
> Poor Reasoning
>
> Impulsive Behaviors
>
> Phobias and Paranoia
>
> Psychosis

At the higher end of the spectrum serious effects develop quickly and are easily observed. This is where intervention becomes necessary if not engaged previously. These can include:

> Withdrawal from Others
>
> Isolation from Work
>
> Escape Behaviors
>
> Pain Numbing
>
> Self-Injury
>
> Suicidal Ideation

Burnout is a spectrum disorder and therefore a process and not an event. It can be prevented at any stage.

Typically people who are out for more than 90 days due to hospitalization and recovery do not return to the same job or even the same employer.

© Jeff Jernigan, PhD, FAIS 2017

LIFE PURPOSE COACHING CENTERS, INTERNATIONAL™
Helping You Know And Fulfill Your Life Purpose

A Prayer of Surrender

Lord,

forgive me

for my petty thoughts and evil ways.

Lift my heart to grander things,

things above,

that I might not disappoint You.

Strengthen me

to serve and love

as a vessel for Your glory.

Let Your true nature shine through me

for the fulfillment of Your purpose.

Bury me in the humility of Your grace

that I might experience joy

in simple obedience.

© Jeffrey T. Jernigan, Scriptural Roots of Ministry, 1987, used by permission

THIN SPACES PRAYERS

As we continue on this journey of listening to God and asking God to restore our souls to live a life of healing, health, and wholeness, join us in praying the following prayers.

> Lord, give me revelation about the meaning of your ways.
> Bless me with an understanding heart so I can passionately know and obey your truth.
> Guide me into the paths that please you, for I take delight in all your ways.
> Cause my heart to bow before your words of wisdom and not to the wealth of this world.
> Help me turn my eyes away from illusions so that I pursue only that which is true. Drench my soul with life as I walk in your paths.
> These six prayers are from Psalm 119: 33–37 NIV.

> Lord, may my faith be greater than my fears.
> Help me to trust you with every part of my life and participate in your great purposes for my life.
> May peace and solace reign in our hearts, for we need inner strength to follow your ways.
> Bless me with a calm spirit, clear thinking, and resilience to move forward.
> When we are in distress, may we call on your name immediately to heal and restore us.
> May I trust God in this season with my whole heart and life.

BIBLIOGRAPHY

This is a list of sources we used in research for this book. Some of them may be helpful to your continued exploration of wholeness in Christ. Others may have been footnoted in the book, and this will provide author and publisher information. For more information, you can reach us at jjernigan@hiddenvaluegroup.com, njernigan@hiddenvaluegroup.com, www.hiddenvaluegroup.com, or nancyjernigan.com.

Allen, J. *Get Out of Your Head: Stopping the Spiral of Toxic Thoughts*. Waterbrook, 2020.

Amen, D. *The End of Mental Illness*. Tyndale, 2020.

Amthor, F. *Neurobiology for Dummies*. John Wiley and Sons, 2014.

Anderson, N. Jacobson, M. *The Biblical Guide to Alternative Medicine*: Regal 2003.

Banaji, M. Greenwald, A. *Blind Spot: Hidden Biases of Good People*: Delacorte Press 2013.

Barnhill, C., Editor. *A Year with Dietrich Bonhoeffer*: Harper Collins, 2005.

Barton, R. *Pursuing God's Will Together: A Discernment Practice for Leadership Groups*: IVP Books 2012.

Barton, R. *Strengthening the Soul of Your Leadership: Seeking God in the Crucible of Ministry*: IVP Books 2008.

Bernard of Clairvaux. *The Love of God*: Multnomah Press 1983.

Bevere, L. *Without Rival: Embrace Your Identity and Purpose in an Age of Confusion and Comparison*: Revell, 2016.

Bullinger, E. *Figures of Speech Used in the Bible*: Baker Book House 1988.

Coleman, L. *50 Years Lost in Medical Advance: The Discovery of Hans Selye's Stress Mechanism*: American Institute of Stress Press 2021.

Cozolino, L. *The Neuroscience of Human Relationships: Attachment and the Developing Social Brain*, 2nd Edition: Norton and Company, 2014.

Erikson, M., Editor. *Readings in Christian Theology*, Vol 1–3: Baker 1979, 1985, 1988, 2003, 2015.

Evans W. *The Great Doctrines of the Bible*: Moody 1992.

Farrell, D. *Examples and Principles of Psychology in the Bible*: Redemption Press 2010.

Foster, R. *Celebration of Discipline*: Harper & Roe 1978, 1988, 1998, 2007, 2018.

Gordon, S. *Quiet Talks on Prayer*: The Christian Library 1984.

Jernigan, J. *The Power of a Loving Man*: Broadman and Holman Publishers 2006.

Jernigan, J. *Contentment*: Contentment Magazine, American Institute of Stress Spring 2021.

Jernigan, J. *Dreams, Nightmares, and Disturbed Sleep*: Combat Stress Magazine, American Institute of Stress Fall 2021.

Jernigan, J. *Physical Ramifications of Prolonged Stress*, Contentment Magazine, American Institute of Stress Fall 2020.

Keller, P. *A Shepherd Looks At Psalm 23*: Zondervan 1991.

Keller, T. *The Freedom of Self-Forgetfullness: The Path To True Christian Joy*: 10Publishing, UK 2012, 2013, 2015, 2017.

Lockyer, H. *All the Miracles of the Bible: The Supernatural in Scripture, Its Scope and Significance*, Zondervan 1961, 1964, 1965, 1973.

Lynn, S. McConkey, K. Editors. *Truth in Memory*: Guilford Press 1998.

McMillen, S. Stern, D. *None of these Diseases*: Revell, 1963, 1984, 2000.

Metzger, B. *Textual Commentary on the New Testament*, 3rd Edition: United Bible Society 2005.

Miller, R. *The Millennium Matrix: Reclaiming the Past, Reframing the Future of the Church*: Jossey-Bass 2004.

Miller, R. Jernigan, J. *Strategy in Re-Building: Principles to Building Post-Traumatic Growth*: Mindshift, 2020.

Muller, W. *Sabbath: Restoring the Sacred Rhythm of Rest*: Bantam Books 1999.

Murray, I. *Jonathan Edwards, A New Biography*: Banner of Truth 1988.

Nockels, C. *Living the Life You Long For*: Multnomah 2021.

Noonan, B. *Advances in the Study of Biblical Hebrew and Aramaic: New Insights for Reading the Old Testament*: Zondervan 2020.

Nouwen, H. *Making All Things New: An Invitation to the Spiritual Life*: Harper Collins 1981.

Ortlund D. *Gentle and Lowly: The Heart of Christ for Sinners and Sufferers*, Crossway 2020.

Rees, E., Jernigan, J. *Tilt: Building Hope, Empowering Leaders*, Abingdon Press 2009.

Ross, H. *Every Day Bias: Identifying and Navigating Unconscious Judgments in Our Daily Lives*: Rowman and Littlefield 2020.

Scazzero, P. *Emotionally Heathy Spirituality: Unleash a Revolution in Your Life in Christ*: Thomas Nelson 2006.

Sinek, S. *Start With Why*: Portfolio Penguin 2009, 2011.

Staton, T. *Praying Like Monks, Living Like Fools*: Zondervan, 2022.

Summers, R. Sawyer, T. *Essentials of New Testament Greek*: Broadman & Holman 1950, 2019.

Tozer, A. *A Cloud By Day, A Fire By Night: Finding and Following God's Will for You*: Bethany House, Re-Release 2019.

Van Der Merive, C. *A Biblical Hebrew Reference Grammar, 2nd Edition*: Bloomsburg 2017.

Willard, D. *The Divine Conspiracy: Rediscovering Our Hidden Life in God*: Harper Collins, 1998, 2018.

ENDNOTES

1   1 Kings 19:11–13.
2   Isaiah 30:21.
3   Isaiah 43:16–19.
4   Isaiah 42:16.
5   Ephesians 2:1–22.
6   Colossians 1:15–20; Numbers 14:21.
7   Jeremiah 2:13.
8   Genesis 1:27..
9   Romans 8:6.
10 W. Evans, *The Great Doctrines of the Bible* (Moody, 1992).
11 John 14:1–31
12 1 Corinthians 2:12
13 Matthew 18:20; 1 Corinthians 3:16
14 Ephesians 5:1–21
15 Philippians 2:1; 2 Corinthians 13:14
16 Philippians 4:6–7
17 James 3:13–18
18 Ortlund D., *Gentle and Lowly: The Heart of Christ for Sinners and Sufferers*, Crossway 2020
19 Exodus 34:6–7
20 Matthew 11:29
21 John 1:12
22 1 Corinthians 12:13
23 See Romans 12 and 1 Corinthians 12, 13, and 14
24 Romans 12:3–8
25 1 Corinthians 12:18–20

26 1 Corinthians 12:7; 12–30; Ephesians 4:12
27 2 Timothy 3:16–17
28 Ephesians 4:11–13
29 Deuteronomy 10:12; Mark 12:30; Luke 10:27.
30 A term used in the Old Testament book of Haggai describing a passionate self-examination, not just mere reflection.
31 Not his real name
32 Galatians 5:16–18
33 Hebrews 5:14 – Training our senses
34 Matthew 28:20
35 Romans 12:1–2
36 Mark 4:9–13
37 Foster, R., Celebration of Discipline: Harper & Roe 1978, 1988, 1998, 2007, 2018
38 John 10:10
39 Isaiah 48:17–18; John 7:17
40 Hebrews 12:3
41 Jeremiah 7:27–28
42 Ephesians 1:17–18
43 1 Thessalonians 5:19
44 Acts 17:10–11
45 Psalm 46:1
46 Joshua 4:1–10
47 Joshua 4:24
48 Matthew 6:1–4
49 Luke 2:19
50 Lynn, S., McConkey, K., Editors, *Truth in Memory*: Guilford Press 1998
51 Matthew 8:5–13
52 Matthew 9:1–8
53 Jeremiah 29:11
54 Genesis 17:1
55 Genesis 21:5
56 John 7:17
57 Psalm 119:105
58 1 Kings 19:11–13
59 Job 4:12–16
60 Jeremiah 29:11–13
61 Isaiah 43:19

62 Matthew 11:1–6

63 Jernigan, J., *Dreams, Nightmares, and Disturbed Sleep*: Combat Stress Magazine, American Institute of Stress, Fall 2021

64 Kaufman D, Meyer H, Milstein, M, *Clinical Neurology for Psychiatrists, Sleep Disorders, Eighth Edition*: Elsevier 2013

65 Lynn, S, McConkey K, Editors, *Truth in Memory, Expectancy Effects in Reconstructive Memory*: Guilford Press 1998

66 1 Kings 19:3–9

67 Genesis 18:1–2

68 Mark 9:24

69 Matthew 16:11–12

70 Judges 6:1–10

71 Matthew 1344–45

72 Cunningham, S. et al, *Structural and functional connectivity of the precuneus and thalamus to the default mode network*: Human Brain Mapping 38(2), National Medical Library, 2017

73 Voltz, K., Cramon, D., *What neuroscience can tell about intuitive processes in the context of perceptual discovery: Journal of Cognitive Neuroscience*, 18(12), Dec 2006

74 Acts 17:11

75 John 3:4

76 John 6:44 & 63; Matthew 16:17

77 Hebrews 5:14

78 Matthew 7:7–8

79 Acts 17:22–27

80 Matthew 4:19

81 John 7:17; Psalm 111:10

82 John 6:24

83 Acts 2:42–47

84 See Acts chapters 3 & 4 for the full story.

85 Tozer, A., *A Cloud By Day, A Fire By Night: Finding and Following God's Will for You*: Bethany House, Re-Release 2019

86 Lockyer, H., *All the Miracles of the Bible: The Supernatural in Scripture, Its Scope and Significance*, Zondervan 1961, 1964, 1965, 1973

87 Joel: a Minor Prophet in the Old Testament who illustrates how God uses natural phenomenon over supernatural intervention at times. Other examples are found in Amos 4, Joshua 10, and Isaiah 38.

88 Acts 2:22 "mighty works" literally works of power.

89 Psalm 139:13–16
90 Jernigan, J., *Physical Ramifications of Prolonged Stress:* Contentment Magazine, American Institute of Stress, Fall 2020
91 Hebrews 12:3
92 1 Kings 19:11–12
93 Isaiah 43:19
94 John 14
95 Psalm 23:3
96 2 Corinthians 5:17
97 Matthew 12:15–21
98 Isaiah 42:1–4
99 Isaiah 42 Ellicott's Commentary for English Readers, bibleapps.com
100 John 21
101 1 Peter 2:9
102 Acts 3:19
103 John 3:16, 5:24; 14:6
104 John 20:23
105 John 14:25–27
106 Isaiah 44:28; 45:1; Ezra 1:1–11
107 Jeremiah 25:11–14; 29:10
108 Ezra Chapters 3 and 4
109 Ezra Chapter 5ff
110 Romans 3:23
111 1 Corinthians 15:58
112 Proverbs 2:3–5
113 Job 34:4
114 2 Peter 1:19–21
115 Hebrews 1:1–2
116 Isaiah 50:4–5
117 Romans 8:26
118 Luke 11:1; Matthew 6:1–15
119 John 9:31; 16:23
120 Matthew 6:5–6
121 Psalm 75:6–7
122 John 15:12–17
123 John ch 14, 15, 16
124 1 Thessalonians 1:6
125 Philippians 1:12–13

126 Philippians 4:11–13
127 John 15:7
128 Romans 8:26.
129 Romans 8:28
130 Ephesians 3:12
131 Ephesians 3:20
132 1 Corinthians 2:12
133 John 15:7
134 Hebrews 4:14–16
135 Titus 1:12
136 Acts 12
137 Judy Singer, PhD, Harvard Medical School, 1990
138 Jankowiak-Suida, K, Rymarczyk, K., et al, How we empathize with others: A neurobiological perspective: Medical Science Monitor 2011, 17(1): RA18–24
139 John 16:8–11; John 15:26
140 Roman 8:12–13; John 16:8–11
141 Titus 3:5; 1 Corinthians 2:12
142 Revelations 3:20
143 Matthew 6:33; 7:7
144 Isaiah 55:6; 65:1; cf Roman 10:20
145 John 7:17
146 Ephesians 4:22–24; Colossians 3:9–12
147 Revelation 3:20
148 Numbers 14:21; Habakkuk 2:14
149 2 Corinthians 5:17–21
150 2 Corinthians 5:17–20
151 Matthew 6:33
152 Psalm 139:13–16
153 Hebrews 10, 24–25
154 1 John 2:15–16
155 James 4:18
156 Isaiah 57:14–21
157 John 14:25–27
158 Psalm 143
159 John 16:33
160 1 Timothy 6:6

161 Jernigan, J., *PTSD and the Neurology of Learning*: Combat Stress Magazine, American Institute of Stress, 2021

162 Proverbs 14:12; 16:2; 21:2

163 See chapter 6 for further explanation

164 Philippians 4:6, 7; 1 Peter 5:6

165 Romans 8:28

166 Philippians 4:6

167 Jeremiah 29:11

168 Cozolino, L., *The Neuroscience of Human Relationships: Attachment and the Social Brain, Second Edition*: Norton and Company March 2014

169 John 14:27

170 Ephesians 4:20–24; Colossians 3:5–12

171 John 3:8

172 John 11:1–44

173 Philippians 4:6–7

174 This saying first appeared in writing unattributed in the late nineteenth century. Some have claimed or assigned attribution; however, the author remains unknown.

175 John 14:21

176 John 12:21

177 Luke 19:40

178 Isaiah 43

179 Jeremiah 3:3;14:3–6

180 Isaiah 42:16

181 John 7:17

182 Isaiah 30:15

183 Isaiah 26:3; 41:10

184 Daniel 4:34–35; Acts 17:22–26

185 John 9:1–12

186 Matthew 15:1–20

187 Hebrews 4:12; 2 Peter 1:3–4

188 Hebrews 13:8

189 Jeremiah 15:16

190 Jeremiah 1:4, 11, 13

191 Isaiah 55:11

192 Jeremiah 29:11

193 Jeremiah 18:1–10

Printed in the United States
by Baker & Taylor Publisher Services